SINGA

Travel Guide

2023-2024

A Comprehensive Guide to the City's Top Attractions

Maria Martin

Copyright © 2023 Maria Martin

All rights reserved.

No part of this publication may be reproduced, stored in a retrieval system, or transmitted in any form or by any means, electronic, mechanical, photocopying, recording, or otherwise, without the prior written permission of the copyright owner.

TABLE OF CONTENT

MAP OF BEDOK

MAP OF JURONG EAST

INTRODUCTION

CHAPTER ONE

About Singapore
Singapore's History and Culture
Practical Information for Visitors

CHAPTER TWO

Planning Your Trip
Best Time to Visit Singapore
Budgeting and Expenses
Visa Requirements
Travel Insurance
Packing Tips

CHAPTER THREE

Getting to Singapore
By Air
By Sea
By Land

CHAPTER FOUR

Exploring Singapore
Districts and neighborhoods
Orchard Road
Orchard Road Overview
Marina Bay
Chinatown
Little India
Sentosa Island
Clarke Quay

CHAPTER FIVE

Popular Attractions

Gardens by the Bay

Merlion Park

Botanic Gardens of Singapore

Singapore National Museum

Singapore Zoo

CHAPTER SIX

Hidden Gem

Kampong Glam

Pulau Ubin

Haw Par Villa

MacRitchie Reservoir

CHAPTER SEVEN

Outdoor Activities

Biking and Hiking Trails

Water Sport

Golf Courses

Nature Reserves

CHAPTER EIGHTH

Shopping and entertainment

Shopping Malls

Night Market

Theaters and Shows

CHAPTER NINE

Singaporean Cuisine

Local Delicacies

Hawker Centers and Food Courts

Halal And Vegetarian Options

CHAPTER TEN

Transportation in Singapore

MRT Stands for Mass Rapid Transit

Buses

Singapore Ride-sharing Services

Renting a Car or a Bicycle

Routes for Walking and Cycling

Tips and Safety

CHAPTER ELEVEN

Accommodation Options

Resorts and Hotels

Budget Accommodation

Serviced Apartment

Guesthouses and Hostels

TWELVE CHAPTER

Cultural Etiquette and Tips

Multiculturalism and Respect:

Greetings & Customs

Dress Code

Tipping and Service Charges

Local Laws and Regulations

Safety and Security

Emergency Contacts and Assistance:

CHAPTER THIRTEEN

Special Events and Festivals

Chinese New Year (CNY):

Singapore Food Festival:

Singapore Grand Prix:

Singapore Arts Festival:

CHAPTER FOURTEEN

Useful Phrases and Language Tips

Basic Phrases in Singaporean English

CONCLUSION

MAP OF BEDOK

Bedok: Is Situated in the southeastern part of Singapore, Bedok is a mature residential town with a mix of public and private housing. It has a bustling town center, various recreational facilities, and access to East Coast Park.

MAP OF JURONG EAST

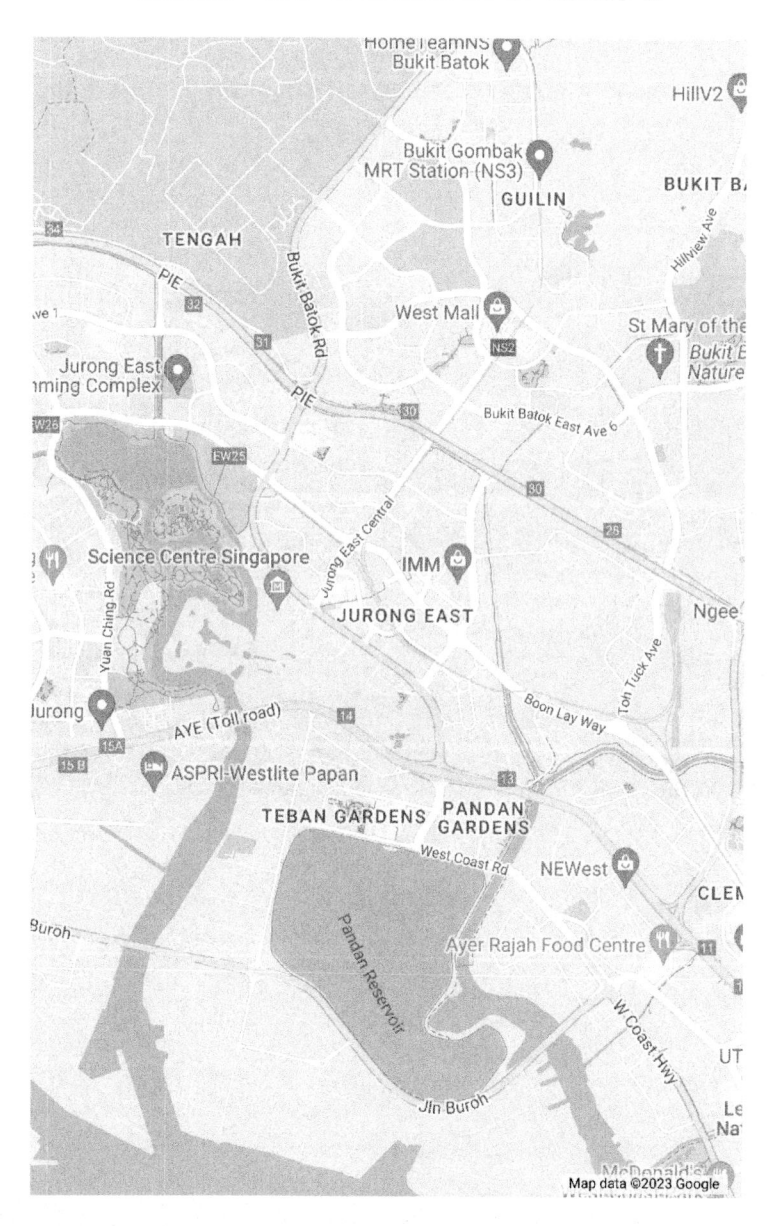

Jurong East: Is Located in the western part of Singapore, Jurong East is a major commercial and residential area. It is known for its shopping malls, office buildings, and the Jurong Lake Gardens.

INTRODUCTION

Welcome to the Singapore Travel Guide 2023, your one-stop shop for information on one of Asia's most fascinating cities. This meticulously curated guidebook will immerse you in the vibrant and dynamic city-state, providing critical information, insider perspectives, and professional guidance to ensure a successful stay.

With its rich cultural tapestry, awe-inspiring architecture, delectable cuisine, and gracious hospitality, Singapore continues to amaze visitors. As you turn the pages of this guide, prepare to embark on a beautiful journey through a city that seamlessly blends heritage and innovation, giving many unique experiences.

Singapore Travel Guide 2023 will be your dependable travel companion, whether you are a first-time visitor or a seasoned traveler. Begin by delving into the city's intriguing history and discovering the cultural influences that shaped its distinct identity. Learn about the city's traditions, customs, and way of life so that you may participate in it more deeply.

The journey then takes you through Singapore's various neighborhoods and districts, each with its distinct personality and charm. Wander the bustling lanes of Orchard Road, Singapore's renowned retail heaven, or take in the futuristic vista of Marina Bay. Immerse yourself in Chinatown's bustling cultural enclave or Little India's vivid colors and smells. From the picturesque Sentosa Island to the hectic waterfront hotspot of Clarke Quay, this book reveals the hidden gems and must-see sights that await you at every step.

Singapore is well-known for its culinary delights, and this book looks deeper into the city's culinary culture. Discover a delectable array of local dishes at bustling hawker centers and food courts, where aromatic aromas blend harmoniously. Furthermore, we highlight traditional dining experiences and recommend famous restaurants where you may sample both local and international cuisine.

The Singapore Travel Guide 2023 provides essential travel information and insights into the city's transportation network to help you navigate this bustling metropolis. We provide comprehensive support to ensure comfortable and enjoyable travel, whether you like to explore via the quick MRT system, a traditional trishaw, or a scenic river cruise.

We provide exciting day tours and excursions to local places outside the city limits, allowing you to immerse yourself in the beauties of Malaysia and Indonesia. Explore the peaceful serenity of Pulau Tioman, the cultural tapestry of Johor Bahru, or unwind on Bintan Island's stunning beaches. These exciting activities are only a short distance away and provide a welcome change of scenery.

Immerse yourself in the Singapore Travel Guide 2023 to discover the real spirit of this great city-state. Singapore has it all, whether you're looking for cultural exchanges, gastronomic delights, natural landscapes, or unforgettable memories. With our expert assistance and recommendations, you can create a unique schedule that suits your interests and objectives.

Set out on an adventure and let the Singapore Travel Guide 2023 be your ultimate guide, transforming your vacation into a remarkable experience you will remember for years. Allow Singapore to entice you, and may this book serve as your passport to an unforgettable adventure.

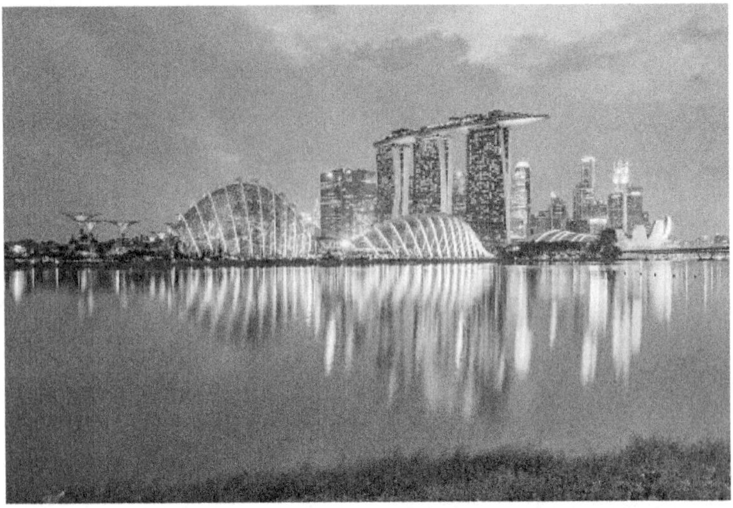

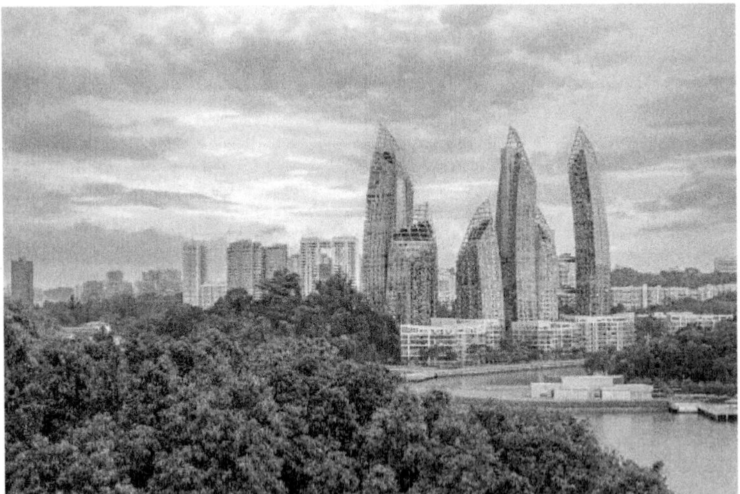

CHAPTER ONE

About Singapore
Singapore's History and Culture

Singapore, located at the Southeast Asia crossroads, has a rich and exciting history that has shaped its vibrant culture and made it the dynamic city-state it is today. Singapore's history is a testament to its people's resilience and dedication, from its humble beginnings as a fishing hamlet to its rise to global economic powerhouse status.

EARLY COLONIAL INFLUENCE AND HISTORY:

Singapore's first human settlement dates back to the third century CE when the island was known as Temasek. It was a bustling trading port, attracting merchants from China, India, and the Arab world. In the 14th century, Singapore was ruled by the Majapahit Empire before falling into decline.

In 1819, Sir Stamford Raffles, an officer of the British East India Company, established modern Singapore. Raffles recognized the strategic importance of the island's location and built a trading post, bringing British colonial power to the island. Under British authority, Singapore became a major economic powerhouse, attracting immigrants from around Asia and beyond.

JAPANESE OCCUPATION AND INDEPENDENCE:

1942 Singapore succumbed to Japanese invaders, beginning a decade of pain and injustice. The occupation had a long-lasting impact on Singaporeans, fueling the desire for self-determination.

After the war, the desire for independence grew more robust, and Singapore declared independence from Malaysia on August 9, 1965. Singapore embarked on a journey of nation-building and progress under the leadership of its first Prime Minister, Lee Kuan Yew.

ECONOMIC REBIRTH AND MODERNIZATION:

As a newly independent nation, Singapore had enormous challenges, such as limited natural resources, a small land area, and a diverse people. On the other hand, Singapore transformed itself into a global economic powerhouse through strategic planning, good governance, and a focus on education and innovation.

Implementing pro-business policies, developing world-class infrastructure, and promoting a skilled workforce enticed international investment, assisting Singapore in becoming a regional financial and business center. It is now regarded as one of the most prosperous countries in the world, with a strong economy and a high standard of living.

PEACE AND CULTURAL DIVERSITY:

Singapore's multicultural community is a vibrant tapestry of different ethnicities, languages, and faiths. The four major ethnic groups are Chinese, Malays, Indians, and Eurasians, who all contribute to the nation's cultural tapestry. Cultural heritage is highly valued, and Singapore is home to various festivals, traditions, and cuisines.

Due to its dominance, Chinese culture is celebrated through events such as Chinese New Year and the Hungry Ghost Festival. The Malay community honors their traditions with festivals like Hari Raya Puasa, while the Indian population celebrates Deepavali and Thaipusam. The blending of cultures has also resulted in a distinct Singaporean identity, reflected in Singlish, a hybrid of English, Mandarin, Malay, and other dialects.

INNOVATION AND HERITAGE PRESERVATION:
While Singapore is known for its gleaming skyscrapers and cutting-edge infrastructure, efforts have been made to preserve its historic sites and cultural heritage. The ethnic enclaves of Chinatown, Little India, and Kampong Glam, with their well-preserved shophouses, temples, and traditional businesses, provide glimpses into Singapore's history.

The National Museum of Singapore, the Asian Civilisations Museum, and the Peranakan Museum all provide opportunities to learn more about Singapore's history and multicultural heritage. These establishments exhibit antiques, exhibitions, and interactive displays that give insight into Singapore's past and future.

Singapore has embraced innovation and technology in recent years, establishing itself as a global leader in finance, smart city solutions, and sustainable development. Gardens by the Bay, a modern playground and natural park, and the world-famous Marina Bay Sands integrated resort demonstrate the city-state's commitment to innovation.

Singapore's history and culture are evolving, with a dynamic balance of preserving its rich legacy and embracing new opportunities. The country's commitment to multiculturalism, social peace, and sustainable development has propelled it into the international spotlight, making it an appealing destination for visitors seeking a unique blend of history and contemporary.

When you visit Singapore, you'll see ancient temples coexisting with rising skyscrapers, local markets and high-end retail malls, and a wide range of cuisines, from street food vendors to Michelin-starred restaurants. Singapore's identity is defined by its ability to honor its past while looking forward—a testament to its people's perseverance, adaptability, and open-mindedness.

Singapore's history and culture will take you by surprise at every turn, whether wandering through Chinatown's colorful streets, admiring the city's skyline's stunning architecture, or tasting its culinary scene's diverse flavors. Prepare to adventure in this fascinating city-state, where old traditions meet new technologies and the past and present coexist happily.

Practical Information for Visitors

1. Visa: You may be required to obtain a visa to enter Singapore, depending on your nationality. Contact your country's embassy or consulate to determine if a permit is required.

2. Currency: The Singapore Dollar (SGD) is the official currency of Singapore. Currency exchange is available at the airport and banks. Credit cards are usually accepted, but having extra cash is always a good idea.

3. Public Transportation: Singapore has an advanced public transportation system comprised of buses, trains, and taxis. The most convenient and cost-effective mode of transportation is the Mass Rapid Transit (MRT) system.

4. Language: The official languages of Singapore are English, Malay, Mandarin, and Tamil. You should have no issue conversing because English is widely spoken and understood.

5. Climate: Due to Singapore's tropical climate, it is hot and humid all year. To stay hydrated, pack light, airy clothing and drink plenty of water.

6. Safety: Singapore is generally a quiet and peaceful country. However, caution should always be exercised. Keep your belongings close to your hand and be aware of your surroundings, especially in crowded places.

7. Culture: Singapore has a diverse culture with a long history and many customs. To respect local norms, dress modestly, remove your shoes before entering a home or temple, and avoid public displays of affection.

IMMIGRATION
SINGAPORE

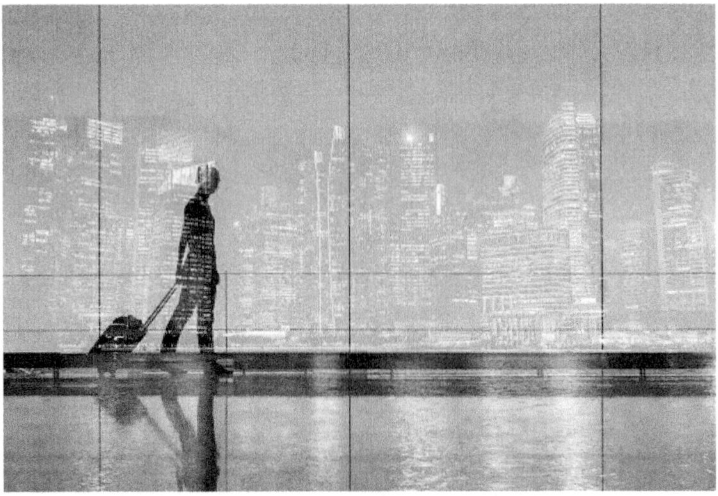

CHAPTER TWO

Planning Your Trip
Best Time to Visit Singapore

Singapore is open all year. However, your interests and activities determine the best time to visit. Here's a look at the seasons and what to expect:

The Dry Season: Dry season in Singapore lasts from January to March, with little or no rain. The weather is lovely and warm, making it an ideal time to experience the city's outdoor attractions. It's also a busy tourist season, so expect more people and rates.

April through June: Singapore's rainy season begins with thunderstorms and showers. The temperature remains warm, but the humidity has risen. If you're on a tight budget, now is a great time to visit because rates are lower than during peak season.

Singapore's wettest months are July and September: With heavy rain and thunderstorms. The weather is hot and humid, but if you don't mind the rain, this is a great time to visit because there are fewer visitors and lower prices.

Singapore's rainy season ends with occasional rain from **October to December:** The weather is more relaxed and less humid, making it an ideal time to visit the city's outdoor attractions. It is also an excellent time to come if you are on a tight budget, as rates are frequently lower than during peak season.

The dry season (January - March) is the best time to visit Singapore to escape the weather and enjoy the city's outdoor attractions. The rainy season (April to September) can provide reduced prices and fewer passengers if you have a tight budget. There is always lots to see and do in Singapore, no matter what time of year you visit!

Budgeting and Expenses

Singapore is widely regarded as one of the most expensive cities in the world, but more is needed to ensure cheap travel there. Here are some budgeting and cost-cutting tips for your trip to Singapore:

Accommodation: Singapore offers various lodging options, from budget hostels to luxury hotels. To save money, consider staying at a hostel or a low-cost hotel. These can be had for as little as $20 per night. If traveling in a group, consider renting an Airbnb or an apartment.

Food: Singapore is well-known for its excellent cuisine, but dining out may be expensive. Look for hawker centers or food courts that provide a variety of local cuisine at low prices to save money. A lunch at a hawker center might cost as little as $3. If you want to treat yourself to a special dinner, go for lunch rather than supper because the prices are usually lower.

Transportation: Singapore has an efficient public transportation system, including buses and trains. Consider purchasing an EZ-Link card, valid on all modes of public transportation. A single journey on the MRT (train) can cost as little as $0.70. Taxis and ride-sharing services are also available at a higher price.

Attractions: Singapore has many attractions, from museums to theme parks. Consider purchasing a Singapore Tourist Pass, which provides unlimited public transportation journeys and discounted admission to numerous attractions. You can buy a one-day, two-day, or three-day pass. Many sites also offer discounted access to students and older people.

Shopping: Singapore is well-known for shopping, but it may be expensive. To save money, look for sales or discounts. Retail malls typically host sales around major holidays such as Chinese New Year or Christmas. You can also get inexpensive souvenirs in hawker zones or markets.

Overall, with some planning and research, visiting Singapore on a budget is possible. If you choose reasonable lodging, eat at hawker centers, take public transportation, and look for bargains, you may enjoy everything Singapore offers without breaking the bank.

Visa Requirements

If you're considering taking a vacation to Singapore, you should know the visa requirements before you go. Here's everything you need to know:

Visa Exemptions: Citizens of a few countries are exempt from obtaining a visa to enter Singapore. The United States, Canada, the United Kingdom, Australia, New Zealand, and various European countries are among them. Consult the Singapore Immigration & Checkpoints Authority (ICA) website if you are unsure whether you need a visa.

Visa Requirements: If you are not exempt, you must apply for a visa before traveling. The purpose of your visit determines the type of visa you need. The most common types of visas are:
- **Visit Visa:** This is for travelers visiting Singapore for less than 30 days.
- **Business Visa:** Business visitors staying in Singapore for less than 30 days.
- **Employment Visa:** This visa is for people who have been offered a job in Singapore and plan to stay.
- **Student Visa:** This visa is for individuals who want to study in Singapore.

To apply for a visa, first, apply to the ICA. You'll need to provide your passport, a passport-sized photograph, and additional supporting documents depending on the type of visa you're using for. The application fee varies according to the type of visa.

If you are currently in Singapore and must stay longer than your visa allows, you can apply for a visa extension. You must provide a valid reason for the extension, such as a medical emergency or unforeseeable circumstances. The application fee for a visa extension is $40.

Overall, it is critical to understand the visa requirements before visiting Singapore. If you are not exempt from needing a visa, apply well before your trip. If you are currently in Singapore and require a visa extension, do so before your visa expires. Following these suggestions, you can enjoy your trip to Singapore without worrying about visas.

Travel Insurance

Singapore can be a terrific destination, but you must be prepared for the unexpected. It is where travel insurance can help. Everything you need to know about Singapore travel insurance is right here:

What is the definition of travel insurance? Travel insurance is a type of insurance that covers unanticipated incidents that may occur while on vacation. Medical issues, vacation cancellations, lost or stolen bags, and other mishaps are examples.

Why Do You Need Travel Insurance in Singapore? While Singapore is a reasonably safe place to visit, risks are always involved. For example, you may become ill or injured in Singapore and require medical attention. Because medical care in Singapore can be expensive, having travel insurance may assist in covering such costs. Furthermore, if your vacation is canceled or delayed due to unforeseen circumstances, travel insurance can help cover the costs of rescheduling or canceling your trip.

What Does Travel Insurance Cover? The coverage provided by travel insurance differs depending on the policy purchased. Some examples of popular styles of coverage are:

- **Medical Coverage:** This covers you if you fall ill or are injured while traveling.

- **Trip Cancellation Protection:** This covers the costs of canceling or rescheduling your trip if it is delayed or canceled due to unforeseen circumstances.

- **Lost or Stolen Luggage Protection:** This covers the expense of replacing lost or stolen luggage.

- **Emergency Evacuation Coverage:** This covers the costs of an emergency medical evacuation if you become critically ill or injured and must be transported to a hospital.

How to Choose Travel Insurance: Examining your specific needs while purchasing travel insurance is critical. For example, if you plan to participate in adventure sports in Singapore, ensure your insurance covers them. You should also consider the duration of your trip, your budget, and the type of coverage you want.

Travel insurance can provide you with peace of mind while in Singapore. If you get the right policy and understand your coverage, you may enjoy your trip without worrying about the unexpected.

Packing Tips

Here are some packing suggestions for your Singapore trip:

1. Light and Breathable Clothing: Due to Singapore's hot and humid climate, light and breathable clothing, such as cotton or linen, is required. You should also bring a light rain jacket or umbrella in case of sudden downpours in Singapore.

2. Comfy Shoes: Because you'll walk a lot in Singapore, comfortable shoes are essential. Sneakers or walking shoes are appropriate, as are beach sandals or flip-flops.

3. Electrical Adapters: Singapore's electrical system is 230V/50Hz; therefore, bring an adaptor if you carry any electrical devices. These may be found in most travel stores and online.

4. Sunscreen and mosquito repellent: In hot and humid weather, the danger of sunburn and mosquito bites increases. To keep yourself safe, bring sunscreen and bug spray.

5. Swimwear: If you intend to visit Singapore's beaches or swimming pools, bring swimwear.

6. Travel documents: Remember to include your passport, itinerary, and other essential documents for your trip.

7. Cash and Credit Cards: Because Singapore is a cashless society, bring your credit or debit card when making transactions. Keeping some cash on hand for small purchases or emergencies is also a good idea.

8. Medications: Bring enough for your visit in their original containers if you use prescription medications. Over-the-counter drugs, such as pain relievers and antacids, should also be included.

9. Camera: Singapore is a beautiful city with many photo opportunities, so bring a camera to document your adventures.

CHAPTER THREE

Getting to Singapore
By Air

Step 1: Choose an Arrival Airport:
Singapore is served by Changi Airport, one of the world's busiest and best-connected airports. Before purchasing your Changi Airport ticket, consider which terminal you will arrive at. Changi Airport has four terminals (T1, T2, T3, and T4), and the one you use depends on your carrier. Check your airline's website or connect with your travel agent to find out which terminal you'll be arriving at.

Step 2: Book Your Flight:
Once you've checked your arrival terminal, it's time to purchase your flight to Singapore. Many airlines fly into

Changi Airport from crucial places across the world. Use online travel businesses, airline websites, or travel agents to discover the most rates and flight selections that fit your preferences and budget. Consider travel time, layovers, and in-flight facilities when selecting your choice.

Step 3: Documentation and Visa Needs:

Make sure you have a valid passport for at least six months from the date you enter Singapore. You may need to obtain a visa before going depending on your nationality. Singapore has visa waiver arrangements with various countries, allowing travelers to enter without a visa for a set amount of time. If your nationality demands a visa, apply early to prevent any last-minute complications.

Step 4: Preparing Departure
Before your flight, take the following precautions:
a) Packing: Check your airline's baggage allowance to eliminate unexpected charges. Pack travel adapters, comfortable clothing, travel-sized toiletries, and any prescriptions that may be needed.
b) Travel Insurance: Consider purchasing travel insurance to protect yourself from unplanned events like flight cancellations, medical troubles, or misplaced luggage.
c) Airport Transfers: Plan your journey from home to the airport ahead of time. Consider employing public transit, hiring a private transfer, or driving yourself. Allow plenty of time to avoid unanticipated delays.
Step 5: Airport Procedures:
When you arrive at the airport, you should follow the following general procedures:
a) Check-In: To complete the check-in process, proceed to the approved check-in counters of your airline. Ensure you have your passport, plane tickets, and any other required travel documentation.

b) Immigration and Security: Proceed to passport control and security screening after checking in. Before passing through security, prepare to remove any electrical gadgets, drinks, or outerwear. Take your passport and boarding pass to immigration.

c) Departure Lounge: Proceed to the departure lounge after passing through security and immigration. Visit duty-free shops, relax in lounges, or grab a bite to eat before flying.

Step 6: In-Flight Experience:

Relax and enjoy your flight to Singapore! Most long-distance flights offer in-flight entertainment, meals, and drinks. Use these luxuries and your flight time to rest, watch movies, or plan your Singapore trip.

Step 7: Arrival in Singapore:

When your jet arrives at Changi Airport, do the following:

a) Immigration and Customs: After disembarking, provide immigration your passport and completed arrival card. Collect your luggage and go through customs according to Singapore's import regulations.

b) Ground Transportation: To go to your hotel, you can choose from several ground transportation solutions, such as taxis, private transfers, or public transportation, based on your preferences and location.

By Sea
Option 1: Cruise ships:
Traveling to Singapore via cruise ship is a popular and quiet choice. Many foreign cruise lines include Singapore as a port of call on their itineraries, allowing passengers to embark or depart. Here's everything you need to know:

Look for trustworthy cruise lines that feature Singapore as a stopover or destination. Examine their itineraries, duration, and amenities to select which best matches your expectations.

Departing Ports: Find the departing port that is most convenient for you. Singapore cruises commonly depart from Hong Kong, Shanghai, Sydney, and Dubai. Consult the cruise line's website or a travel agency to determine the most convenient departure place.

Timetable & Visas: Check the cruise itinerary to confirm that it corresponds to the length of your intended stay in Singapore. Establish if your nationality needs a visa to enter Singapore and plan accordingly.

Onboard Experience: Once onboard, familiarize yourself with the ship's facilities and entertainment options. Take advantage of the services, activities, and culinary options on your cruise to Singapore.

Option 2: Ferries from Other Countries:

If you live in Malaysia or Indonesia, sailing the ferry to Singapore is a natural alternative. Everything you need to know is as follows:

Choose a Ferry Company: Several ferry companies operate regular services between Singapore and adjacent regions such as Batam (Indonesia) and Johor Bahru (Malaysia). Investigate and uncover a dependable operator who fulfills your excursion aims.

Departure Points: Find the departure point that is nearest to you. In Malaysia, significant departure ports include the Stulang Laut Ferry Terminal in Johor Bahru and the

Tanjung Belungkor Ferry Terminal in Tanjung Belungkor. The Batam Centre Ferry Terminal and the Sekupang Ferry Terminal in Batam provide stable connections from Indonesia to Singapore.

Ferry Schedules: Examine the ferry schedules to confirm availability and departure times that meet your journey plans. It is vital to reserve your tickets in advance, especially during peak travel seasons.

Prepare your travel documentation for immigration and customs, including your passport and any required visas. When you arrive in Singapore, follow the immigration and customs procedures at the ferry terminal.

Option 3: Charter or a private yacht:

Arriving in Singapore by private boat or charter is a premium and bespoke solution for individuals wanting a premium and personalized experience. Here are some things to consider:

Yacht or Charter Service: Hire a recognized yacht charter service that offers Singapore cruises. Check that they have travel experience abroad and follow all safety requirements.

Customs and Immigration Clearances: Arrange customs and immigration clearances for entry into Singapore with the yacht charter firm. This stage is vital for assuring compliance with local rules and a smooth admissions procedure.

Singapore has marinas and berthing facilities for private boats. Consider ONE°15 Marina Sentosa Cove or Raffles Marina to dock your yacht conveniently.

Arrival Port: Research the entrance protocols and requirements for your preferred Singapore arrival port. Clear customs and immigration before disembarking.

By Land

Even though Singapore is an island city-state, the bustling metropolis may be accessible by land via neighboring countries. Traveling by land to Singapore offers a once-in-a-lifetime opportunity to witness the varied landscapes, cultures, and experiences along the way. In this guide, we will look at the many routes and transportation possibilities for visiting Singapore by land, giving you vital information and advice for a hassle-free journey.

Route 1 from Malaysia to Singapore:

Malaysia and Singapore share a land border, making it the most accessible alternative for land travel. Here's how to get there:

1-Choose an Entry Point:

There are two main entry points from Malaysia to Singapore:

a) Woodlands Checkpoint: Woodlands Checkpoint is the central admission point for buses, automobiles, and trains in Singapore's northern region. The Causeway, a road and rail link, connects it to Johor Bahru in Malaysia.

b) Tuas Checkpoint: Located on Singapore's western fringes, Tuas Checkpoint operates as an alternate vehicle and bus admission point. Another road connector, the Second Connector, connects it to Iskandar Puteri in Malaysia.

Select a Mode of Transport:

Depending on your interests and convenience, you can choose from the following means of transportation:

a) Bus: Many bus lines connect Malaysia with Singapore, providing a quick and economical form of transit.

Buses leave from Malaysian cities such as Kuala Lumpur, Johor Bahru, and Melaka and arrive at many terminals in Singapore.

b) Train: The KTM Shuttle Tebrau is a train service that connects Johor Bahru's JB Sentral station in Malaysia with Singapore's Woodlands Train Checkpoint. As an alternative to driving, it gives a pleasant and intriguing experience.

c) Private car or Taxi: Hire a private automobile or take a cab from Malaysia to Singapore for a more personalized experience. You gain flexibility and ease by allowing you to build your own timeline.

2-Immigration Clearance:

At the border checkpoints, you must go through immigration clearance. Check that your passport and any relevant visas are ready for scrutiny. Follow the advice of the immigration authorities and complete the relevant papers before continuing your journey.

3-Inspection of Customs and Baggage:

Proceed to the customs division for baggage checks after passing through immigration. Ensure you are informed of Malaysian and Singaporean customs processes to avoid issues. Declare any restricted or dutiable products as necessary.

Route 2: Thailand, Cambodia, and Vietnam to Singapore

While it is a lengthier route, land travel to Singapore is available from surrounding countries such as Thailand, Cambodia, and Vietnam. Here's a high-level overview of your options:

1-Make plans to visit Kuala Lumpur or Johor Bahru:
You must first travel to Malaysia, namely Kuala Lumpur or Johor Bahru, if you are in Thailand, Cambodia, or Vietnam. Depending on your starting point and preferences, you can do this via bus, train, or aircraft.

Take the following route from Malaysia to Singapore:
Follow the procedures above to go from Malaysia to Singapore after arriving in Kuala Lumpur or Johor Bahru. Select your desired entry point and mode of transportation (Woodlands or Tuas Checkpoint).

2-Prioritize stops and overnight stays:
Given the distance, preparing for rest stops and overnight hotels along the way is vital. Assess and identify relevant hotel possibilities based on your itinerary and travel preferences. If traveling from Thailand, consider visiting Malacca (Melaka), Kuala Lumpur, Penang, or Kuala Lumpur if traveling from Cambodia or Vietnam.

Considerations for Three Vehicles:
If you're traveling by car or motorcycle, ensure you have the proper permits, insurance, and driver's licenses for the countries you visit. Educate yourself about each country's road legislation and traffic conditions to secure a safe and comfortable ride.

CHAPTER FOUR

Exploring Singapore
Districts and neighborhoods
Orchard Road

An awe-inspiring assemblage of towering businesses and lovely boutiques met me. The second I entered Orchard Road. Each step along the 2.2-kilometer stretch revealed a fresh shopping heaven, compelling me to study its offerings. I proceeded through the ION Orchard corridors, where well-known luxury names attracted me with their stunning displays.

Ngee Ann City's multi-level shopping wonderland pulled me in with its broad range of boutiques, while Paragon drew me in with its gorgeous assortment of brand names. It was a shopping heaven where imaginations and wishes were perfectly combined.

But Orchard Road is more than simply luxury shopping. It unfolded like a colorful tapestry, integrating entertainment and leisure within its weave. The Singapore Art Museum is a tribute to the city-state's booming arts economy, and its thought-provoking displays drew me in.

I was escorted to a magnificent show at the Esplanade - Theatres on the Bay that transported me to another dimension. I sought escape from the crowded streets and went to the calm Singapore Botanic Gardens, a lush oasis where nature's serenity greeted me. The district's proximity to historical landmarks benefited me in excavating Singapore's rich legacy, bringing richness to my visit.

As my adventure advanced, I visited the culinary zone of Orchard Road, teasing my taste sensations with various delicacies. The neighborhood appealed to my gastronomic aspirations, from the fiery spices of local hawker stalls to the polished masterpieces of Michelin-starred restaurants. I appreciated the vibrant flavors of chili crab, the aromatic notes of laksa, and the delicate aromas of Hainanese chicken rice.

Each flavor told a tale about Singapore's rich cultural background, leaving me wanting more. The Orchard Road Food Festival marked the culmination of my gourmet adventure, with a sensory feast of excellent delicacies from around the world.

My trek down Orchard Road was a tribute to the district's attractiveness as a leading shopping destination. It was more than just a collection of malls and stores; it was an intriguing experience that tickled my senses and interested me.

The fascination of Orchard Road resides not merely in its sumptuous shopping offerings but also in the rich tapestry of entertainment, culture, and gastronomy that weaves its enchantment throughout.

Set off on your trip and let Orchard Road seduce you with a symphony of luxury and magic.

Orchard Road Overview

Orchard Road, located in the heart of Singapore, is a dynamic and famous shopping district that epitomizes the city-state's international nature. Orchard Road is a must-see location for travelers seeking a seamless blend of luxury, culture, and leisure. It is noted for its fancy shopping companies, numerous entertainment possibilities, and extraordinary culinary experiences.

Orchard Road is a 2.2-kilometer-long bustling thoroughfare filled with world-class shopping malls, exquisite boutiques, and flagship stores of well-known multinational brands. Shopaholics will delight in the abundance of options, ranging from high-end designer labels to cutting-edge electronics. At the same time, enthusiastic food lovers may sample a variety of global cuisines and local specialties available at the numerous restaurants, cafes, and food courts scattered around the street.

Shopping Heaven

The retail possibilities on Orchard Road cater to various interests and inclinations, ensuring that every shopper's demands are addressed. From luxury fashion giants like Louis Vuitton and Gucci to trendsetting firms presenting fresh local designers, Orchard Road offers many possibilities. Visitors looking for a one-of-a-kind shopping experience can visit historic malls such as ION Orchard, Ngee Ann City, and Paragon, which feature exclusive collections and flagship retailers. Furthermore, the yearly Orchard Road Christmas Light-Up adds a great touch to the region, creating an attractive ambiance for visitors during the holiday season.

Recreation and leisure

Aside from its commercial attraction, Orchard Road boasts a rich tapestry of entertainment and recreational activities. Art lovers can take in the current exhibits at the Singapore Art Museum or see a performance at the Esplanade - Theatres on the Bay. Travelers opting for a more leisurely experience can take a soothing stroll around the lovely Singapore Botanic Gardens, a UNESCO World Heritage site near Orchard Road. Furthermore, the district's proximity to the Civic District makes historical attractions such as the National Museum of Singapore and Fort Canning Park conveniently accessible.

Delights in the Kitchen

The culinary scene on Orchard Road caters to all tastes, featuring great fine dining venues and exquisite street food experiences. Michelin-starred restaurants, celebrity chef cafes, and authentic local hawker centers offer a diversity of culinary delights. Singapore's hallmark meals, such as chili crab, laksa, and Hainanese chicken rice, will delight your taste buds, or you can indulge in other cuisines that reflect the city's worldwide tapestry. The iconic Orchard Road Food Festival, hosted irregularly, exhibits Singapore's rich culinary legacy, allowing visitors to sample various flavors and gastronomic experiences.

Because of its central location and robust connectivity, Orchard Road is easily accessible via public transit, particularly the M.R.T. system.

In Singapore, visitors can shop tax-free, and many malls provide tourist privileges and discounts.

Throughout the year, Orchard Road organizes various events and performances, ranging from fashion shows and art exhibitions to music festivals, adding life and excitement to the region.

Engaging with local tour guides or downloading Orchard Road-specific smartphone apps can enrich the experience by delivering insights into hidden treasures, discounts, and special offers.

Visitors are recommended to visit during the week to escape the weekend crush and make the most of their time in the region.

Marina Bay

Marina Bay, in the heart of Singapore, is a beautiful waterfront zone symbolizing the city-state's modernity, ingenuity, and dynamic vitality. Marina Bay is a must-see destination for travelers looking for an excellent experience, showcasing a magnificent blend of architectural marvels, lush green areas, exquisite hotels, world-class food, and known attractions. This comprehensive tour will cover everything a discerning tourist needs to know about Marina Bay, from its intriguing sights to its thriving nightlife.

Landmarks of Notoriety:

Marina Bay is home to various prominent landmarks that have come to characterize Singapore's skyline. These are some examples:

a) Marina Bay Sands: This world-famous integrated resort comprises three towering hotel towers topped by a gravity-defying rooftop SkyPark with spectacular city views. Marina Bay Sands also includes a world-class casino, upscale shopping boutiques, and a wide choice of culinary pleasures.

b) Gardens by the Bay: Gardens by the Bay, a masterwork of horticulture and sustainable architecture, enchants travelers with its towering Supertrees, bright flower domes, and cloud forests. The Gardens is a calm oasis amid the city, giving a reprieve for nature enthusiasts and those interested in botany.

b) ArtScience Museum: The ArtScience Museum, fashioned like a lotus flower, is a spellbinding venue that mixes art, science, culture, and technology in a new and engaging way. It includes a changing roster of world-class exhibitions that present various subjects while promoting creativity.

Recreation and Entertainment:

Marina Bay provides a plethora of leisure and recreational possibilities for tourists of all ages:

a) Marina Bay Sands Skypark: Take an exciting journey to the top of Marina Bay Sands to find the Skypark. Take in the stunning views of Singapore's skyline, swim in the famed infinity pool, or drink a refreshing cocktail at the rooftop bar.

b) Marina Bay Circuit: Motorsport lovers can see the exhilarating Formula 1 Singapore Grand Prix held annually at the Marina Bay Street Circuit. Witness the world's fastest vehicles hurtling through city streets under a stunning canopy of lights.

b) Spectacular Light and Water Shows: Take advantage of Marina Bay Sands' intriguing light and water shows. The daily Wonder Full presentation blends water, lasers, lights, and music to create an exciting sight.

Nightlife and Dining:

Marina Bay boasts a fantastic dining scene, with a varied assortment of gastronomic experiences to satisfy all tastes:

a) Celebrity Chef Restaurants: The Marina Bay Sands relish the gastronomic delights of renowned chefs. CUT by Wolfgang Puck, Waku Ghin by Tetsuya Wakuda, and Bread Street Kitchen by Gordon Ramsay all offer creative flavors and exquisite cuisine.

b) Quayside Dining: Stroll down Marina Bay Sands' waterfront promenade to uncover the busy dining enclave. There's plenty for everyone, from trendy pubs and casual cafes to fine dining restaurants.

c) Rooftop Bars: Relax and enjoy stunning city skyline views from one of Marina Bay's rooftop bars. Sip exquisite cocktails while indulging in the exciting atmosphere of Singapore's nightlife.

Chinatown

Chinatown, located in the lively city-state of Singapore, is a mesmerizing district rich in history, cultural depth, and gourmet delights. With its distinct blend of Chinese heritage and modern urbanity, Chinatown offers a variety of experiences for visitors wishing to immerse themselves in the city-state's multicultural fabric. This crucial guide will analyze the highlights, attractions, and practical tips for a memorable trip through Chinatown's lovely streets.

Landmarks and Rich Heritage:
Chinatown is entrenched in history, keeping Chinese roots while embracing modern concepts. Here are some must-see attractions:

a) Thian Hock Keng Temple: Immerse yourself in the magical aura of Singapore's oldest Hokkien temple. Admire its elaborate architectural components, peaceful courtyards, and gorgeous sculptures devoted to various deities.

b) Buddha Tooth Relic Shrine and Museum: Learn about Buddhist culture while revering the sacred relic held within this lovely shrine. Explore the museum to learn about the history and ideas of the religion.

c) Sri Mariamman Temple: Admire this Hindu temple dedicated to the goddess Mariamman's bright Dravidian architectural style. Witness religious events and magnificent sculptures reflecting mythical Hindu legends.

Festivals and Cultural Experiences:

Chinatown has a wealth of cultural activities that engage tourists in its lively traditions:

a) Chinatown Heritage Centre: Travel back in time and learn about Singapore's early Chinese immigration. The center offers insight into their struggles, objectives, and contributions to the nation's growth.

b) Festivals: Visiting during holidays such as Chinese New Year or Mid-Autumn Festival allows you to observe colorful processions, exquisite decorations, and many cultural acts that bring Chinatown to life.

c) Street Markets: Visit the crowded street markets on Pagoda Street and Smith Street for great traditional crafts, trinkets, and delicious street cuisine. Negotiate with vendors and taste Hainanese chicken rice and bak kut teh (pork rib soup).

Gastronomic Treats:

Chinatown is a foodie's dream, with an eclectic combination of cuisines and culinary traditions:

a) Hawker Centers: Visit Chinatown Complex or Maxwell Food Centre for inexpensive and authentic local cuisine. From the numerous merchants, enjoy popular foods such as char kway teow (stir-fried noodles) and satay (grilled skewered pork).

b) Heritage Eateries: Visit long-standing gourmet institutions that have endured time. Try the famous chili crab at a seafood restaurant or the delicious dim sum at Chinatown's iconic restaurants.

c) Traditional Tea Houses: Relax in a quiet tea house, where you can sip a cup of fragrant Chinese tea and learn about the art of tea appreciation while enjoying old-world charm.

Practical Information for Visitors:
Keep the following practical things in mind to make the most of your visit to Chinatown:

a) Getting about Public Transit: Such as the M.R.T. (Mass Rapid Transit) or buses, makes navigating Chinatown easy. Wear comfortable shoes because walking is the best way to explore the neighborhood.

b) Cultural Sensitivity: When visiting religious sites or participating in cultural events, respect local norms and traditions. Dress modestly and conform to any standards or constraints set by the specific places.

c) Street etiquette: Because Chinatown can get crowded, be aware of your valuables and stick to essential street manners. When photographing, avoid blocking pedestrian pathways and be respectful of others.

Little India

Little India, located in the heart of Singapore, is a bustling and culturally diverse area that provides a thorough immersion into the customs, flavors, and colors of the Indian subcontinent. Little India captures the spirit of Indian culture while thriving contentedly amid Singapore's cosmopolitan setting, with its vibrant streets, majestic temples, delicious spices, and colorful enterprises. In this comprehensive guide, we will cover everything a tourist to Little India needs to know, from its significant landmarks to practical advice for an engaging visit.

Cultural Relics:
Little India is home to a wealth of cultural landmarks that reflect the Indian community's rich past and traditions:

a) Sri Veeramakaliamman Temple: Dive into the mystical ambiance of this exquisite Hindu temple devoted to the goddess Kali. Admire its beautiful sculptures, brilliant hues, and religious rites that offer insight into Indian religious customs.

b) Sri Srinivasa Perumal Temple: Explore this Hindu temple dedicated to Lord Vishnu's beautiful Dravidian-style architecture. Marvel at the gopuram (entry tower)'s gorgeous sculptures and engage in the festivities during religious feasts.

c) Little India Arcade: The Little India Arcade offers a colorful shopping experience. Discover many businesses providing traditional Indian apparel, jewelry, handicrafts, and spices. Allow the brilliant colors and scents to transport you to the bustling streets of India.

Delights in the Kitchen:

Little India is a gastronomic wonderland that tantalizes the taste buds with its unusual and tasty cuisine:

a) Must-Try Cuisine: Sample classic Indian meals, including biryani, dosa, samosa, and butter chicken. South Indian classics like idli, vada, and masala dosa are at the neighborhood's numerous cafes and hawker booths.

b) Spice Shops: Visit the aromatic spice shops in Little India to find a broad selection of spices, herbs, and sauces that flavor Indian cuisine. Engage with knowledgeable store owners who can share their knowledge of traditional Indian cuisine.

c) Indian Sweets: A range of Indian sweets, such as gulab jamun, jalebi, and barfi, can satisfy your needs. These tasty nibbles are often created with milk, sugar, almonds, and aromatic spices.

Festivals and Cultural Encounters:
During holidays, Little India comes alive, showing the vibrant customs and celebrations of the Indian community:

a) Deepavali: Attend the Festival of Lights, one of the most prominent Hindu festivities in Little India. Observe the streets with dazzling lights, exquisite decorations, and riotous cultural acts.

b) Thaipusam: Witness the stunning Thaipusam parade, in which devotees carry complicated kavadis (burdens) as penance. During this annual festival, the rhythmic rhythms of drums and singing create an exciting environment.

b) Cultural Performances: Participate in traditional music and dance performances that emphasize the diverse art forms of Indian culture. Check out the schedules of places like the Indian Heritage Centre for exciting performances.

Practical Information for Visitors:
Consider the following practical recommendations to make the most of your visit to Little India:

a) Getting Around: Public transportation is readily available in Little India, with the Little India M.R.T. station providing a convenient entry point. Consider wandering around the region to immerse yourself in its vivid surroundings completely.

b) Cultural Etiquette: Observe local customs and religious practices when visiting temples or indulging in cultural events. Dress modestly and take off your shoes when necessary. Before shooting holy locations, ask permission.

b) Street Shopping: Bargaining is frequent in the stores and stalls of Little India. Practice your bartering skills while remaining respectful and friendly.

Sentosa Island

Sentosa Island, located just off the coast of Singapore, is a tropical sanctuary that offers a broad choice of activities for visitors looking for sun-soaked beaches, exhilarating attractions, and immersive entertainment.

Sentosa Island, with its magnificent shoreline, abundant foliage, and world-class resorts, offers guests the opportunity to enjoy various activities and relaxation. This exhaustive guide will reveal all a visitor needs to know about Sentosa Island, from its beautiful scenery to practical tips for a wonderful visit.

Beaches and Outdoor Recreation:

Sentosa Island offers a mix of gorgeous beaches and outdoor activities for both relaxation and adventure seekers:

a) Palawan Beach: Soak up the sun on the golden sands of Palawan Beach, which is noted for its family-friendly ambiance and gorgeous blue waters. To reach the southernmost point of continental Asia, cross the suspension bridge.

b) Siloso Beach: Siloso Beach offers a busy beach atmosphere with water sports, beach volleyball, and beach parties. Try kayaking or stand-up paddleboarding, or relax with a cool cocktail at a beach tavern.

c) Nature treks & trails: Explore the island's natural charms via various courses and tours. Stroll along the Sentosa Boardwalk, visit the Sentosa Nature Discovery, or take a relaxing nature walk along the Imbiah Nature Trail.

Attractions and Theme Parks:

Sentosa Island is noted for its world-class amusement parks and activities for people of all ages:

a) Universal Studios Singapore: At Universal Studios Singapore, you can immerse yourself in a world of cinematic enchantment.

In this iconic theme park, you may ride thrilling coasters, meet popular characters, and enjoy live concerts.

b) S.E.A. Aquarium: Explore the depths of marine wonders at the S.E.A. Aquarium, one of the world's largest aquariums. See interesting aquatic life, such as sharks, rays, and brilliant coral reefs.

c) Adventure Cove Waterpark: Escape the tropical heat with adrenaline-pumping water slides, a lazy river, and a snorkeling lagoon at Adventure Cove Waterpark. Get up close and personal with aquatic life as you snorkel alongside magnificent species.

Cultural and Historical Treasures:
Sentosa Island is more than just beaches and activities; it also provides insight into the island's cultural and historical significance:

a) Fort Siloso: Visit Singapore's sole rebuilt coastal fort, Fort Siloso. Discover the island's military history through interactive exhibits, artillery displays, and underground tunnels.

b) Madame Tussauds Singapore: Visit Madame Tussauds Singapore to see the lifelike wax figures of your favorite celebrities, historical figures, and sports stars. Take one-of-a-kind images and participate in interactive activities.

c) Images of Singapore LIVE: Step back in time and explore Singapore's rich legacy and cultural variety at

Images of Singapore LIVE, a multimedia journey exhibiting the nation's history, traditions, and achievements.

Practical Information for Visitors:

Consider the following practical advice to ensure a pleasant and comfortable vacation to Sentosa Island:

a) Transportation: Take the Sentosa Express monorail, the Sentosa Boardwalk, or a taxi to Sentosa Island. Alternatively, use the extensive bus network or the Sentosa Cable Car for a scenic journey.

b) Attractions Packages: To save money and enjoy access to various attractions, consider purchasing bundled attraction tickets or Sentosa Fun Passes.

c) Food and Shopping: Sentosa Island provides many food alternatives, from casual seaside cafes to fine-dining places. Discover unique shopping experiences at Resorts World Sentosa and the Quayside Isle.

Clarke Quay

Clarke Quay, located along the famed Singapore River, is a busy and lively location that offers a variety of activities for people searching for a mix of entertainment, food, and nightlife. Clarke Quay is a significant place that showcases the city-state's particular attraction, with its magnificent seafront, busy streets, and a broad assortment of establishments. In this complete tour, we will discover all a visitor needs to know about Clarke Quay, from its attractions and dining options to practical advice for a memorable visit.

Famous Attractions:

Clarke Quay is home to numerous well-known attractions that showcase its historical and cultural significance:

a) Read Bridge: Admire the architectural splendor of Read Bridge, a historical relic that connects Clarke Quay to the picturesque Boat Quay. From this vantage point, you may snap stunning views of the Singapore River and the city's cityscape.

b) Asian Civilizations Museum: At the Asian Civilizations Museum, you may immerse yourself in Asia's rich cultural past. Explore various antiques, art, and exhibitions that provide insights into the region's history and traditions.

c) River Cruises: Take a calm river boat down the Singapore River, which affords panoramic views of the city's sights and skyline. Select between antique bumboat cruises and modern river taxis for a thrilling excursion.

Dining Opportunities:

Clarke Quay is a gourmet wonderland, offering a varied choice of dining alternatives to delight every palate:

a) Riverside Dining: Enjoy al fresco dining at waterfront eateries along the Singapore River. You may savor excellent dishes from traditional Singaporean food to world flavors while overlooking the river and the lively ambiance.

b) Quayside Dining Concepts: Explore Clarke Quay's numerous dining alternatives, from casual cafes to fine-dining places. Experience diverse cuisines, fusion meals, and unusual culinary concoctions in a bright and exciting setting.

c) Nightlife and Bars: Clarke Quay changes into a lively nightlife district as night falls. Discover a range of bars, pubs, and clubs that provide live music, entertainment, and a vibrant party environment.

Activities and Entertainment:

Clarke Quay features a variety of leisure opportunities and activities to satisfy a wide range of interests:

a) G-MAX Reverse Bungy: G-MAX Reverse Bungy is an adrenaline-pumping activity for thrill fans. Strap in and prepare to be propelled into the air for a gravity-defying adventure with stunning views of the surrounding area.

b) Trishaw Rides: Take a classic Trishaw ride around Clarke Quay's streets. Allow your trishaw puller to be your guide as you tour the neighboring sites and soak in the neighborhood's vibrant atmosphere.

Clarke Quay is well-known for its vivid street performances, live music, and cultural shows. Be amazed by outstanding artists and entertainers as they demonstrate their skills and talents on the crowded streets.

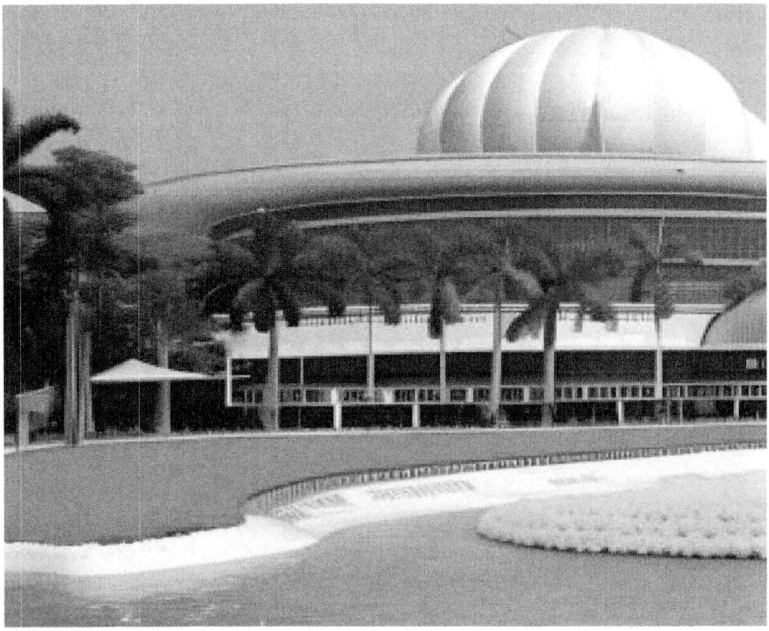

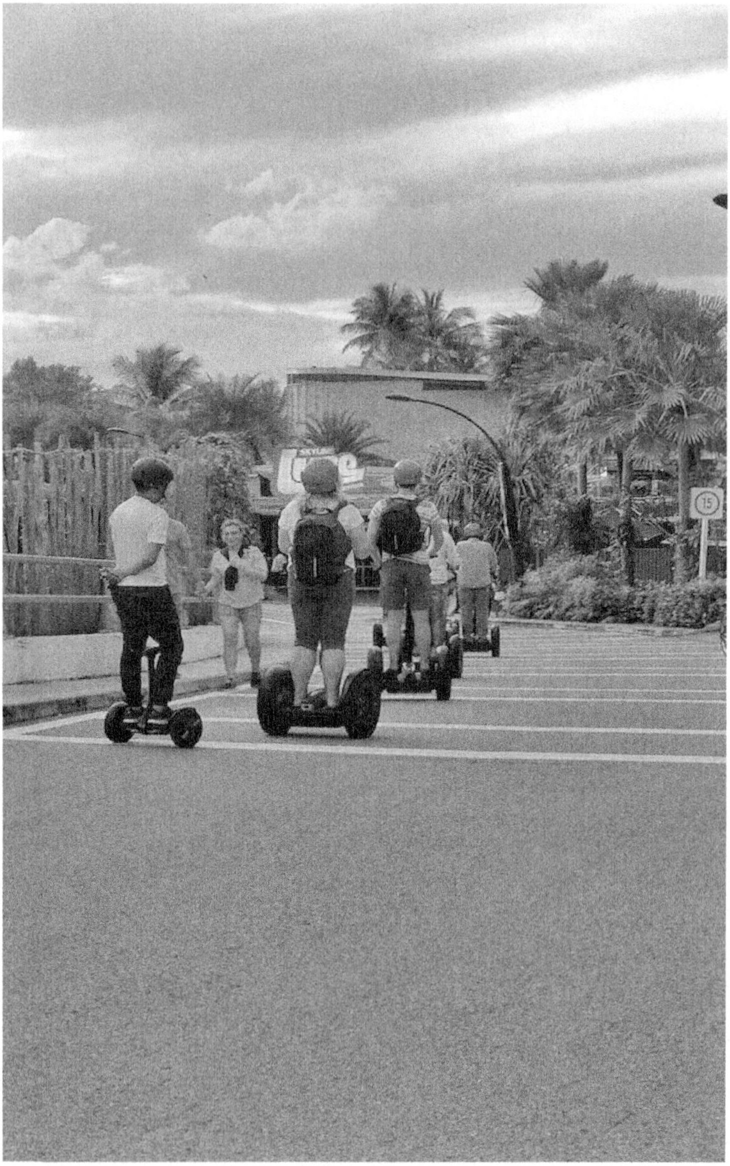
15

CHAPTER FIVE

Popular Attractions
Gardens by the Bay

Gardens by the Bay is a world-renowned horticultural destination in the heart of Singapore. This spectacular garden complex, encompassing 101 hectares, gives visitors a remarkable blend of nature and modernity. Gardens by the Bay has become a must-see attraction for locals and tourists worldwide, thanks to its awe-inspiring design, diverse plant life, and ecological approaches.

Architectural Design

Gardens by the Bay's design acknowledges Singapore's ambition to develop a green and sustainable metropolis. The park is separated into three sections: Bay South, Bay East, and Bay Central. The largest area, Bay South, has two world-renowned conservatories, the Flower Dome and the Cloud Forest, which highlight various plants from diverse temperate zones. Another remarkable feature of Bay South is the Super tree Grove, which comprises gigantic tree-like structures covered with vertical plants and serves aesthetic and valuable purposes.

Biodiversity and Plant Life

Gardens by the Bay features an excellent range of global flora. The Flower Dome, the world's largest glass greenhouse, recreates the cool-dry Mediterranean atmosphere by showcasing a diversity of plants such as olive trees, cacti, and vivid blooming species. The Cloud Forest, on the other hand, replicates the cool-moist conditions seen in tropical highland regions and displays a diverse assortment of ferns, orchids, and bromeliads.

Aside from the conservatories, the Gardens by the Bay outer gardens are also spectacular. Through themed landscapes, the heritage Gardens pay homage to Singapore's distinct cultural past, while the World of Plants shows a variety of uncommon and exotic plant species. Other attractions that provide tranquil surroundings for guests to unwind and appreciate nature's splendor include the Dragonfly Lake and the Sun Pavilion.

Innovation and sustainability

Gardens by the Bay is well-known for its attention to environmental preservation and sustainability. The Super trees, a vital component of the gardens, demonstrate this commitment. These vertical gardens function as both beautiful components and crucial ecological engines. They provide shade, collect rainwater, and are equipped with photovoltaic cells that harness solar energy, decreasing the gardens' dependency on artificial lighting and air conditioning.

Water conservation is an essential issue at Gardens by the Bay. The gardens use advanced technology to collect, process, and recycle rainwater for irrigation, minimizing dependency on freshwater supplies. Visitors can also explore the magnificent Dragonfly Lake, a freshwater ecosystem that fosters biodiversity and works as a natural filtering system.

Amenities and experiences for guests

Gardens by the Bay presents a variety of experiences for visitors of all ages and interests. Aside from the gorgeous flora, the gardens feature a range of activities and exhibitions throughout the year, such as flower shows, cultural festivals, and horticultural demonstrations. Outdoor recreational activities, such as strolling and cycling along the waterfront promenade, are also offered to guests.

Gardens by the Bay offers several amenities to make your visit more comfortable. Dining options range from basic cafes to gourmet restaurants, with cuisines satisfying every taste. The Gardens Shop sells souvenirs, books, and gardening-related products for customers to take home as souvenirs. Guided tours and audio guides are also available to improve the entire experience and provide extra information on the garden's features.

Merlion Park

Merlion Park, located in the heart of Singapore's Marina Bay, is a well-known and picturesque sight that draws visitors worldwide. The mythical Merlion statue, a mythological monster with the head of a lion and the body of a fish, can be found in this waterfront park. Merlion Park, as a symbol of Singapore's history, culture, and national identity, gives tourists a once-in-a-lifetime opportunity to immerse themselves in the city-state's legacy while enjoying breathtaking views and a bustling atmosphere.

History and Importance

The Merlion is essential in Singaporean culture and serves as a symbol of the country's roots. The Merlion was developed in 1964 as an emblem for the Singapore Tourism

Board, representing the city-state's link to the ocean and its history as a fishing hamlet. The name "Merlion" is a mix of "me" (meaning sea) and "lion," which reflects the Malay word for lion, "Singa."

The Statue of the Merlion

Merlion Park's centerpiece is the vast Merlion monument, which rises 8.6 meters tall and weighs 70 tons. This vast sculpture catches the imagination with its larger-than-life presence and mystical allure. The statue has a lion's head, a magnificent mane, and a fish's body that spreads gently into the surrounding oceans.

Visitors can inspect the monument up close, marveling at its numerous elements and appreciating the artistry that went into its production. It is a popular photographic backdrop, allowing visitors to preserve their memories of Singapore against the stunning Marina Bay panorama.

Views and surroundings that are scenic
In addition to the spectacular Merlion monument, Merlion Park affords panoramic views of Marina Bay and its neighboring surroundings. Tourists can enjoy the modern architectural marvels that dominate Singapore's skyline from this vantage point, such as the landmark Marina Bay Sands integrated resort and the magnificent ArtScience Museum. The park's beachfront position also provides a quiet ambiance, suitable for a stroll or a moment of calm in the center of the metropolis.

Tips & Amenities for Visitors
When planning a trip to Merlion Park, remember the following ideas to make the most of your time there. The park is always open to the public, allowing visitors to explore it at their leisure. It is easily accessible by public

transit, and parking facilities are nearby for those who drive.

The park provides numerous amenities to ensure the satisfaction of guests. Restrooms and drinking water are provided nearby, giving for a stress-free visit. Carrying sunscreen, a hat, and appropriate walking shoes is advisable while touring the region throughout the day.

Attractions in the Neighborhood

Merlion Park is conveniently positioned near several other well-known sights, giving it an excellent starting point for further exploration. Visitors can stroll to the neighboring Marina Bay Sands complex, which provides world-class shopping, dining, and entertainment. With its famed Supertrees and stunning conservatories, the adjacent Gardens by the Bay gives a great garden experience.

Botanic Gardens of Singapore

The Singapore Botanic Gardens, located in the heart of Singapore, provides a tranquil getaway and a tribute to the city-state's commitment to preserving nature's treasures. It was founded in 1859 and is one of the world's oldest and most famous tropical gardens. The gardens, which cover 82 hectares, offer a vast range of flora, serene landscapes, and educational activities, making it a must-see destination for nature enthusiasts, families, and anybody seeking refuge from the city.

Gardens and Flora

The Singapore Botanic Gardens offer over 10,000 plant varieties, including rare and endangered species. The National Orchid Garden, the gardens' crown gem, presents a stunning display of orchids of varied colors, shapes, and sizes. It houses the world's largest orchid display, with over 1,000 species and 2,000 hybrids, including the famed Vanda Miss Joaquim orchid.

Visitors can visit themed gardens that emphasize various plant species and locations. The Healing Garden shows plants with therapeutic powers, while the Fragrant Garden soothes the senses with its fragrant petals. The Evolution Garden studies the evolution of plant life on Earth, while the Ginger Garden showcases a vast diversity of ginger species. The Rainforest Garden provides an immersive experience replicating a tropical rainforest's sights and sounds.

Conservation and Natural Heritage
Recognizing the value of its floral resources, Singapore Botanic Gardens was named a UNESCO World Heritage Site in 2015. It acts as a living lab for plant research, conservation, and teaching. The gardens actively participate in scientific research and partner with foreign institutes to study and conserve plant species.

The Jacob Ballas Children's Garden is a significant conservation project because it tries to inspire a love of nature in young visitors. It offers interactive displays, educational activities, and play spaces to boost children's understanding and respect for wildlife.

Amenities and Recreational Activities
Aside from its botanical magnificence, the Singapore Botanic Gardens offers a variety of leisure activities and services to guests. The spacious lawns and picnic places are excellent for relaxing and family gatherings. Visitors can

take leisurely walks or participate in running and fitness activities along the many pathways that loop through the gardens.

The Symphony Lake, covered with lovely water lilies, organizes concerts and performances by local and international performers. These events offer a one-of-a-kind opportunity to witness live music in breathtaking surroundings, resulting in a harmonic marriage of nature and culture.

The gardens offer a variety of dining alternatives for people looking for gastronomic delights, ranging from modest cafes to upscale restaurants. Visitors can have supper while immersed in the garden's tranquility or indulge in a delightful afternoon tea at one of the excellent cafés.

Visitor Tips and Information

The Singapore Botanic Gardens are open to the public from 5 a.m. to 12 a.m. daily, allowing travelers to savor the gardens' beauty at their leisure. The gardens are free to enter, with a nominal fee for specialty areas like the National

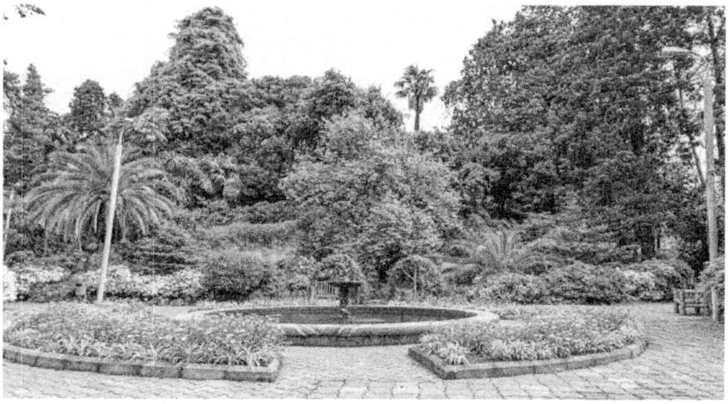

Orchid Garden

Guided tours are available to enhance the visit, providing insights into the gardens' history, plant collections, and conservation programs. Visitors can also explore at their own pace by downloading self-guided audio tours.

Because the gardens demand significant exploration, dressing comfortably and wearing walking shoes is best. Sunscreen, caps, and bug repellent are vital, especially in tropical areas.

Singapore National Museum

The National Museum of Singapore is a fascinating institution that highlights Singapore's rich history, culture, and heritage. As the country's oldest museum, it occupies a special place in people's hearts and presents a complete narrative that follows Singapore's evolution from its early origins to the present day. The National Museum of Singapore, with its massive collections, immersive exhibitions, and engaging activities, provides visitors with a unique opportunity to dive into the nation's past and develop a more excellent knowledge of its identity.

Architecture and History

The National Museum of Singapore is located in an architectural masterpiece that effortlessly mixes the old and the new. Initially erected in 1887 as the Raffles Library and Museum, the structure has undergone m
any restorations and extensions to become the well-known landmark it is today. Its neo-Palladian architecture contains enormous Corinthian columns, a dramatic dome, and

beautiful detailing, culminating in a visually magnificent landmark representing the museum's historical significance.

Collections and Exhibitions

The museum showcases a variety of exhibitions that highlight Singapore's history and culture. Visitors can explore a variety of subjects and times that create the nation's narrative, from permanent galleries to temporary exhibitions.

The Singapore History Gallery takes travelers on a trip from the 14th century to the current day.

. Visitors can trace Singapore's growth from a small fishing town to a booming cosmopolitan city-state through immersive displays, antiques, multimedia presentations, and interactive exhibits.

The Life in Singapore: Surviving Syonan Gallery is a poignant exhibition that dives into the terrible years of the Japanese occupation of Singapore during World War II, providing a deeper understanding of Singaporeans' perseverance and the impact of war on the nation.

Furthermore, the museum holds temporary exhibitions on various topics, such as art, culture, and contemporary concerns. These performances present unique viewpoints and insights into Singapore's burgeoning artistic and cultural scene.

Events and Programs

The National Museum of Singapore offers many exciting programs and events for individuals of all ages and interests. Visitors can take guided tours that provide in-depth information on the museum's assets and displays. These trips offer unique insights into Singapore's history and legacy, enriching the experience.

In addition, the museum organizes public discussions, workshops, and cultural performances to promote Singapore's unique character. These events allow passengers to mingle with experts, artists, and performers, giving them a deeper grasp of the country's history.

Amenities for Visitors

The National Museum of Singapore offers several conveniences to make your stay more comfortable and enjoyable. The museum's Café Melba features a variety of gastronomic options, from light snacks to complete meals, allowing visitors to recharge while enjoying local and foreign cuisines. The Museum Label Shop presents a

carefully curated range of souvenirs, books, and exciting things inspired by Singapore's history and culture.
Useful Information
The museum opens at 10 a.m. to 7 p.m. Every day, with additional hours on Fridays. Admission to special exhibitions may be paid. However, general admission to the museum is free for Singaporeans and permanent residents.
The National Museum of Singapore is strategically positioned in the city center and is easily accessible by public transit. It is also within walking distance of other cultural and historical attractions, making it a good starting place for learning about Singapore's history.

Singapore Zoo

As I walked through the zoo's gates, I felt a surge of exhilaration and expectation. The air was filled with a symphony of animal sounds, from the joyous chirping of birds to the distant roar of lions. The first exhibit that attracted my eye was the Fragile Forest, an excellent site that transported me to the Middle of a tropical jungle. Walking down the winding road, I was surrounded by lush foliage, towering trees, and flowing waterfalls. Lemurs dangled from branch to limb while bright butterflies buzzed about me, creating a great environment. It was as though I'd walked into a beautiful jungle.

Continuing my tour, I entered the Primate Kingdom, where cheeky orangutans swung effortlessly among the treetops, their funny antics bringing smiles to visitors' cheeks. The Reptile Garden nearby featured a range of writhing snakes and fascinating animals, each with its own unique story to tell.

As I traveled through the Great Rift Valley of Ethiopia exhibit, I became captivated by the sights and sounds of Africa. The enormous savannah extended before me as I gazed at zebras' grace, lions' majestic majesty, and cheetahs' incredible speed. It was as if I'd been transported to the heart of the African jungle.

The event, however, still needs to finish there. The icy allure of the Frozen Tundra beckoned. In this Arctic beauty, I stared in astonishment as gorgeous polar bears swam over the crystal-clear streams. The vision was mesmerizing and humbling—a view into a world different from mine.

Then came the moment I had been anticipating: my encounter with the gentle giants of the Wild Africa zone. Giraffes browsed happily, their long necks extending towards the tallest branches. The gigantic rhinoceroses basked in the sunlight, emanating might and endurance. The elephants captivated my heart with their sparkling stare and compassionate disposition. Seeing these beautiful creatures up close was a gift, and I couldn't help but feel a profound connection to the natural world.

Aside from its visually spectacular exhibits, the Singapore Zoo is severely dedicated to conservation and teaching. I was intrigued and motivated by the zoo's earnest attempts to rescue endangered animals and assist in worldwide conservation projects. The zoo created a true passion for animals and a sense of duty toward our endangered ecology through interactive activities, guided tours, and educational exhibits.

As the day drew to a conclusion, I found myself pondering on the fantastic experience I had done. The Singapore Zoo profoundly impacted me and opened my eyes to the beauty and diversity of our natural environment. It was a place where stories came to life, animals told their experiences, and visitors like myself could become a part of a more remarkable story—the story of conservation, appreciation, and the shared obligation to safeguard the riches that nature has bestowed upon us.

I left the zoo with a memory of the magnificent animals I had seen and a renewed desire to make a difference. The Singapore Zoo narrative will live on in my heart as a reminder of the power of nature, the significance of conservation, and the boundless possibilities within our grasp.

The Singapore Zoo is a world-class zoological park that provides tourists with a one-of-a-kind and immersive wildlife experience. The zoo, located among lush foliage, is noted for its distinctive and naturalistic displays, conservation activities, and educational programs. The Singapore Zoo, focusing on animal welfare and environmental sustainability, provides an informative and delightful experience for visitors of all ages.

Animal Encounters and Exhibits

The Singapore Zoo is home to a varied assortment of species from throughout the world. The exhibits are designed to resemble natural surroundings and provide ample area for animals to roam and thrive. Visitors can get up close and personal with nature's wonders, observing interesting species in conditions that mirror their native habitats.

The Fragile Forest, an immersive exhibit that recreates the ecology of a tropical rainforest, is one of the zoo's main points. Visitors can journey through a stunning habitat with free-roaming wildlife like lemurs and flying foxes. The Primate Kingdom exhibits a range of primates, including orangutans and gibbons, while the Reptile Garden displays reptiles worldwide.

Visitors visiting the Great Rift Valley of Ethiopia exhibit are introduced to African wildlife such as zebras, lions, and cheetahs. The Frozen Tundra exhibit offers a view into the Arctic ecology, with polar bears as the significant feature. The Wild Africa zone transports guests to the savannah, where they may observe spectacular animals such as giraffes, rhinoceroses, and elephants.

Animal performances and feedings are organized throughout the day, allowing visitors to learn more about the animals and watch their natural habits. These encounters, ranging from feeding sessions with orangutans to participation displays with sea lions, provide insight into the animals' life while promoting conservation consciousness.

Education and conservation

The Singapore Zoo is deeply committed to conservation and environmental education. The zoo tries to promote awareness about the importance of wildlife preservation and inspire visitors to take action through various programs and projects.

The Wildlife Protection Program is dedicated to protecting and reproducing endangered species, partnering with international organizations, and participating in global conservation activities. The zoo actively supports species reintroduction into the wild, assuring the long-term survival of threatened animals.

Visitors can learn about animal conservation and biodiversity through educational programs and guided excursions. The Rainforest Kidzworld is a particular area for children that incorporates interactive displays, a petting zoo, and educational activities that encourage environmental awareness.

Amenities & Experiences for Visitors

The Singapore Zoo offers a variety of amenities to ensure a comfortable and delightful visit. Numerous dining alternatives, including cafés and restaurants, offer a variety of cuisines to accommodate a wide range of tastes. Picnic spaces and designated rest areas provide convenient places for travelers to unwind and enjoy their surroundings.

Guests can opt for several animal activities and behind-the-scenes tours for a completely immersive experience. Customers can engage with creatures such as lemurs, orangutans, and elephants while directed by experienced personnel.

Useful Information

The Singapore Zoo is open daily from 8:30 a.m. to 6:00 p.m. It is recommended that guests arrive early to make the most of their visit and prevent crowds. The zoo is well-served by public transit, and enough parking is available for those who prefer to drive.

Because the zoo is so extensive, dressing comfortably and wearing walking shoes is vital. Sunscreen, caps, and bug repellent are essential, especially in tropical areas.

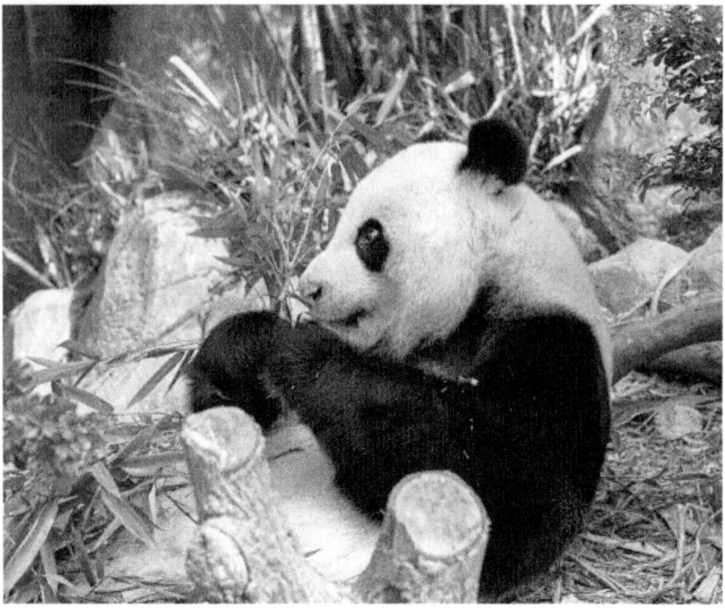

CHAPTER SIX

Hidden Gem
Kampong Glam

Kampong Glam is a lively and culturally varied area in the heart of Singapore that amazes visitors with its historical elegance and unique blend of influences. Kampong Glam has a particular feeling of history and ingenuity due to its rich history as a Malay and Arab enclave. Kampong Glam gives an immersive experience that exhibits Singapore's global fabric, from its spectacular architectural gems to its bustling streets with tantalizing fragrances and active enterprises.

History and heritage

Kampong Glam's history extends back to the early days of Singapore's foundation. Johor Sultan Hussein Shah erected his royal residence nearby, and the city evolved from a fishing town to a busy metropolis. The massive Sultan Mosque, a beautiful landmark with a significant Islamic style, houses relics of its famous past.

Exploring the tiny passageways of Kampong Glam uncovers a treasure trove of heritage structures. The shophouses' colorful façade and ornate ornamentation offer a look into the area's architectural past. Many of these structures have been entirely repaired and remodeled, and they now house a swarm of fashionable cafes, boutiques, and art galleries, bringing fresh vitality to the neighborhood.

Culture and Culinary Delights
Kampong Glam is a cultural melting pot with varied races, cuisines, and artistic expressions. Arab Street is a lively boulevard, a textile and art enthusiast's dream. Its boutiques feature a colorful range of fabrics, rugs, and handicrafts, immersing tourists in the rich tapestry of Arab and Islamic culture.
The region is also a gastronomic joy thanks to its availability of cafés and food merchants. Kampong Glam tempts the senses with various flavors and smells, from traditional Malay food to Middle Eastern pleasures. Visitors can experience aromatic spices, delicious satay, and traditional Arab street cuisine like "kueh lapis."

Fascinating Facts
Apart from the well-known Sultan Mosque, Kampong Glam includes a variety of significant structures. The Malay Heritage Centre takes you on a fascinating trip to Singapore's Malay population's history and traditions. Visitors can learn about the Malays' customs, arts, and contributions through multimedia exhibitions and exciting displays.
The Aliwal Arts venue is a creative location for art lovers that showcases modern art, performances, and cultural events. It features exciting exhibitions, music events, and theatrical performances and serves as a platform for budding artists.
The Haji Road, a busy and narrow street lined with colorful murals and modern businesses, gives a memorable shopping experience. Tourists can find one-of-a-kind

clothing, accessories, and independent enterprises in this region, making it a favorite destination for fashionistas and those seeking one-of-a-kind memories.

Festivals and Special Events
Kampong Glam comes alive during the Christmas season and cultural activities. The annual Hari Raya Bazaar is a bustling market that runs during Ramadan, where visitors can soak up the festive ambiance, enjoy traditional Malay cuisine, and shop for Ramadan presents. The Kampong Glam Arts Festival highlights the artistic flair of the neighborhood with art installations, performances, and seminars.

Helpful Information
Public transit is an alternative because Kampong Glam is adjacent to the Bugis M.R.T. station. The area is best explored on foot, allowing tourists to take in the gorgeous scenery and discover hidden jewels at every turn.

Visit Kampong Glam during the week or early in the morning to avoid crowds. Exploring the region at your leisure provides a more immersive experience, allowing you to interact with friendly stores and people willing to share their experiences and views.

Pulau Ubin
Ubin is located in the Pacific Ocean. It is a picturesque island off Singapore's northeastern coast that gives a calm retreat from city life. Pulau Ubin, famed for its pristine beauty and rustic appeal, is a paradise for nature enthusiasts, outdoor explorers, and history buffs. With its lush forests, stunning beaches, and traditional kampong

(village) environment, Pulau Ubin gives a one-of-a-kind and immersive experience that transports guests back in time.

Ways to Get There
The travel to Pulau Ubin is an adventure in itself. Visitors can take a short ferry from Changi Point Ferry Terminal to the island to take in the spectacular views of the surrounding waterways. When guests arrive on the island, they may leave the city scene behind and enjoy its natural splendor.

Trails for Wildlife and the Natural Environment
Pulau Ubin is a nature lover's delight, with well-preserved pathways flowing through lush woods, mangroves, and wetlands. The island's various habitats sustain a diverse assortment of flora and wildlife.

Chek Jawa, a wetland ecosystem rich in unusual species, is a must-see. Visitors can explore the intertidal flats at low tide and witness various marine life, such as crabs, starfish, and seashells. Visitors can see birds, mudskippers, and other wetland species from the boardwalks and towers, allowing panoramic views of the surrounding mangroves.

Hiking and bicycle routes on Pulau Ubin allow tourists to immerse themselves in the island's scenic interior. The Puaka Hill Summit Trail leads to a vantage point that affords panoramic views of the island and its adjacent islets. The Sensory Trail gives guests a unique experience by allowing them to engage their senses through touch, scent, and sound while wandering through the peaceful woodland.

Pulau Ubin offers the beauty of a typical kampong, with rustic wooden cottages, village temples, and friendly residents that reflect the socioeconomic character of the island. By exploring the Kampong region, tourists can learn about the island's history and immerse themselves in its lovely atmosphere.

The Ubin Living Lab tells visitors about the island's history and culture. Through interactive exhibitions and installations, visitors can enter a reproduction of a 1960s kampong house and learn about the island's early settlers and their ways of life.

Cultural and Recreational Activities

Pulau Ubin offers various activities to meet a wide range of interests. Renting a bicycle is a popular alternative for individuals who prefer leisurely exploring the island. By riding through the twisting roads and paths, tourists may immerse themselves in the natural splendor and feel the freedom of outdoor adventure.

Other popular sports that allow guests to explore the island's beaches, mangroves, and hidden bays include kayaking and paddleboarding. Anglers can cast their lines at specified fishing sites and unwind while angling in nature's embrace.

Helpful Information

Visitors to Pulau Ubin should carry sunscreen, bug repellent, and drinking water. Outdoor activities demand comfortable gear and sturdy boots. Confirming ferry schedules in advance is crucial, as the number of journeys may fluctuate.

Haw Par Villa

Haw Par Villa, located in the heart of Singapore, exhibits the Aw brothers' inventiveness and vision. This fascinating theme park takes tourists on a weird journey through mythology, folklore, and moral concepts. With its stunning statues, bright dioramas, and stunning displays, Haw Par Villa delivers a one-of-a-kind experience that mixes art, culture, and moral instruction.

History and Origins
In 1937, the Aw brothers, Aw Boon Haw, and Aw Boon Par, erected Haw Par Villa to advertise Tiger Balm, their family's well-known medicine. The park, formerly known as "Tiger Balm Gardens," symbolized the Aw brothers' humanitarian aims and desired to impart Chinese culture and moral values.

Moral and Mythical Characters on Display
The park's main feature is an extensive collection of over 1,000 statues and dioramas depicting scenes from Chinese mythology, folklore, and tales. Each sculpture is skillfully carved and shows various personalities, including deities and heroes, mythological creatures, and historical figures.

The "Ten Courts of Hell" are well-known near Haw Par Villa. This lively and often beautiful performance describes the many levels of the afterlife as taught by Chinese tradition. Visitors are brought through the penalty zones, packed with wonderfully carved statues portraying the consequences of various sins and crimes. The Ten Courts of Hell are a constant reminder of the significance of moral behavior and belief in karmic retribution.

Other intriguing installations await visitors who explore the park, such as the Journey to the West portion, which brings the iconic characters from the Chinese literary classic to life. The dioramas show the Monkey King's and his entourage's journeys, providing a glimpse into this timeless story of bravery and wisdom.

Survival and Transformation of Culture

Over the years, Haw Par Villa has undergone many restorations. Initially, it was primarily utilized for moral education and cultural inquiry. It is a distinct tourist destination highlighting Singapore's aesthetic and cultural history.

The park's inherent beauty has been preserved while new components and interactive displays have been added. Guided tours, cultural performances, and storytelling sessions allow the opportunity to learn more about the park's rich past.

Helpful Information

The Haw Par Villa M.R.T. station, as is public transportation, is nearby. The park is available to the public and free of charge, allowing visitors to enjoy its attractions at their leisure. Specific interests, like the "Ten Courts of Hell" exhibit, may charge entry.

Because the park involves walking and touring, visitors should dress comfortably. Because the park provides limited cover in some locations, it's a good idea to bring sun protection, such as hats and sunscreen.

MacRitchie Reservoir

The reservoir at MacRitchie Reservoir is a tranquil retreat away from the rush and bustle of daily life, tucked among the lush vegetation of downtown Singapore. With its peaceful streams, excellent trails, and plentiful animals, it is a shelter for nature lovers, fitness enthusiasts, and those wanting a quiet vacation. Whether you're searching for a stroll, a daring treetop tour, or a close encounter with wildlife, MacRitchie Reservoir promises an immersive and exhilarating experience.

The Environment Around the Reservoir

The MacRitchie Reservoir is an important water catchment area for Singapore, but it is much more than that. The vast body of water, surrounded by thick forests and rolling hills, produces a breathtaking environment that feels like a world removed from the metropolis.

Kayaking, canoeing, and paddleboarding are popular leisure activities at the reservoir. Visitors can hire equipment or join guided tours to explore the peaceful waters and picturesque surroundings.

Walking pathways and a treetop trek

The MacRitchie Reservoir is well-known for its well-maintained network of walking routes that appeal to folks of all fitness levels and interests. The 3.5-kilometer MacRitchie Nature Trail is the most popular, which encircles the reservoir. Tourists can take rests along the trail to absorb the beauty, see wildlife, and unwind.

For those wishing for a more adventurous experience, the TreeTop Walk is the highlight of MacRitchie Reservoir. Visitors can obtain a bird's-eye view of the woodland canopy from this 250-meter-long suspension bridge. For guests, walking among the treetops and absorbing the sights and sounds of nature is a beautiful experience. Please remember that the TreeTop Walk may sometimes be closed for maintenance, so check ahead of time.

Biodiversity and wildlife

Because of its unique flora and fauna, MacRitchie Reservoir is a paradise for nature lovers and animal fans.

Visitors can view monkeys and monitor lizards, squirrels, and various bird species in the neighboring woodlands.

The interpretive boardwalk on the MacRitchie Nature Trail allows visitors to learn more about the area's unique biodiversity. The educational component of the tour is reinforced with information panels that provide insights into the diverse plant and animal species that dwell in this area.

Helpful Information

Public transit is easily accessible to MacRitchie Reservoir, with bus stops near the entrance. For those who prefer to drive, there is also a parking lot. The park is open from early morning to late evening, allowing people to enjoy the tranquil ambiance at various times of the day.

Dressing comfortably and wearing appropriate footwear when walking or trekking is vital. Water, insect repellant, and sunscreen are essential, especially in hot and humid weather. Visitors are asked to obey park guidelines and keep the surroundings clean to preserve the natural beauty of MacRitchie Reservoir.

CHAPTER SEVEN

Outdoor Activities
Biking and Hiking Trails

Singapore is known for its sophisticated architecture and urban conveniences, but it also has many biking and hiking pathways that allow visitors to experience nature's magnificence. Outdoor enthusiasts can explore varied landscapes, witness wildlife, and engage in physical activity on these trails, which range from lush rainforests to seashore walks. Singapore has a path to suit your hobbies and fitness level, whether you love biking or trekking.

East Coast Park is one of Singapore's most popular outdoor destinations, with a beautiful 15-kilometer beachfront bicycle and walking route. With palm-fringed beaches, dense greenery, and panoramic sea views, this track is ideal for a leisurely bike or quiet walk. Along the way, guests can find amenities such as rental stores, food outlets, and rest stops, making it a comfortable and pleasurable experience for everyone.

The island of Ubin

Pulau Ubin, a rustic island off the northeastern coast of Singapore, is a haven for nature lovers and thrill seekers. A cycling and hiking network winds through the island's dense forests, mangroves, and small settlements. Rent a bicycle to explore the island's beautiful countryside, visit stunning spots like the Chek Jawa wetlands, or hike to the Puaka Hill Summit for panoramic views. Pulau Ubin offers a trip back in time and the chance to reconnect with nature.

MacRitchie Reservoir has a parking lot.

MacRitchie Reservoir Park, located in the heart of Singapore, has an extensive path system popular with cyclists and pedestrians. The park's walkways wind through beautiful rainforests, providing opportunities to observe wildlife and relax in nature's peace. Hikers can ascend the famous TreeTop Walk, a suspension bridge with panoramic views of the forest canopy, while mountain bikers can explore the park's mountain biking circuit. MacRitchie Reservoir Park is famous for outdoor enthusiasts looking for a peaceful and scenic getaway.

The South's Ridges

The Southern Ridges is a network of interconnecting paths in Singapore's southern region that traverse various parks and natural reserves. This road offers a one-of-a-kind blend of rich greenery, elevated walkways, and breathtaking views. Mountain bikers and hikers can visit Mount Faber Park, the Henderson Waves (the tallest pedestrian bridge in Singapore), and the Forest Walk. The Southern Ridges is a fantastic option for anyone looking for variety and a breathtaking travel experience.

Singapore is home to the Bukit Timah Nature Reserve.

Bukit Timah Nature Reserve is a natural wonderland in the heart of Singapore. The reserve contains Bukit Timah Hill, Singapore's highest point, and challenging hiking trails lead to the summit. The paths go through beautiful woodlands, providing opportunities to see a variety of plant and animal species. Nature lovers can also explore the nearby Dairy

Farm Nature Park, which has several hiking paths, including the lovely Wallace Trail.

Helpful Information

Before embarking on any riding or hiking trail in Singapore:
- Check the weather conditions.
- Bring extra water.
- Wear appropriate footwear and clothing.
- Use insect repellent if necessary.

Some courses may have limited operating hours or require authorization for specific activities, so check beforehand.

Water Sport

Kayaking and stand-up paddleboarding

Kayaking and paddleboarding are two popular water activities that allow users to explore the waterways of Singapore at their leisure. Explore the tranquil waters of Singapore's reservoirs, such as MacRitchie Reservoir and Lower Seletar Reservoir, or head to the beach to visit East Coast Park and Sentosa Island. Whether you're a novice or a seasoned paddler, these sports allow you to enjoy the peace of nature while still receiving a low-impact workout.

Jet Skiing and Water Jetpacking

For those wishing for a more scary experience, jet skiing and water jetpacking deliver an adrenaline rush on the water. Several coastal locations may provide jet ski rentals, allowing riders to race through the waves and explore the beach with a sense of freedom and adventure. Another option is water jetpacking, which involves putting on a jetpack and soaring above the water propelled by high-powered water jets. These high-octane activities offer a unique perspective of Singapore's coastline and an unforgettable adventure.

Wakeboarding and waterskiing

Wakeboarding and waterskiing are high-speed sports that need agility and balance. Come to Singapore Wake Park on the city's eastern outskirts for an unforgettable wakeboarding experience. The park has cable systems that transport riders around a lake, allowing them to do leaps, stunts, and aerial feats. Waterskiers might find alternatives in some coastal regions and private clubs. These activities are ideal for those looking for an adrenaline-pumping aquatic adventure.

Scuba Diving and Snorkeling

Scuba dive or snorkel to experience a new world beneath Singapore's abundant marine life. Pulau Hantu, an outlying island, offers excellent diving and snorkeling opportunities due to its stunning coral reefs and diverse marine life. Divers of all levels can rent equipment and go on guided tours to discover Singapore's underwater wonders. Snorkelers can also enjoy the shallow seas at various coastal locations, including Sisters' Islands and Lazarus Island, where visitors can see colorful marine species in their natural habitat.

Helpful Information

Safety should be a top priority when participating in water sports activities in Singapore. All safety laws must be followed, sufficient safety equipment must be worn, and weather and water currents must be monitored. Beginners can take classes or join guided tours to ensure a safe and enjoyable experience.

Water sports equipment rentals and guided excursions are available at various coastal and reservoir areas and specialty water sports establishments. Reservations must be made in advance to ensure your preferred time slots, especially during peak seasons.

Golf Courses

Singapore is home to the Sentosa Golf Club.

Sentosa Golf Club, located on the beautiful Sentosa Island, is a well-known golfing venue that has hosted international events. The championship courses at the club are the Serapong Course and the New Tanjong Course. The

Serapong Course is famous for its challenging layout and is regarded as one of Asia's best golf courses. The New Tanjong Course has a more forgiving topography while offering a fun round of golf. Sentosa Golf Club offers an unparalleled golfing experience with breathtaking views of the South China Sea.

Laguna National Golf & Country Club is near Laguna Beach, California.

Laguna National Golf & Country Club is a popular golf course in Singapore's east. The club has two championship courses: the Masters Course and the Classic Course. Andy Dye's Master's Course is a challenging course with international contests. It's famous for its intricate bunkering and undulating fairways. Peter Thomson's Classic Course features tree-lined fairways and water hazards for a more traditional parkland-style play. Laguna National Golf & Country Club, with its exceptional facilities and rich golfing tradition, is a must-see for golf enthusiasts.

The Marina Bay Golf Course

Marina Bay Golf Course, located in downtown Singapore's heart, provides a unique golfing experience. This public golf course creates a one-of-a-kind setting by combining a challenging layout with stunning views of the city skyline. The system features large fairways, strategically placed bunkers, and water hazards, making it a test for all skill-level golfers. Players can unwind at the clubhouse after a round of golf and gaze out over Marina Bay. Marina Bay Golf Course provides accessibility and a fantastic golfing experience in an urban oasis.

Singapore Island Country Club is a country club on the island of Singapore.

Singapore Island Country Club (SICC), established in 1891, is one of the city-state's oldest and most well-known golf clubs. The club's four championship courses are the Bukit Course, the Island Course, the Lake Course, and the New Course. Each course offers a unique golfing experience, with diverse scenery and difficulty levels. The Bukit Course is known for its undulating terrain and breathtaking views, while the Lake Course features water hazards and strategically placed bunkers. SICC provides a one-of-a-kind golfing experience that is enhanced by first-rate amenities and services.

Tanah Merah Golf Club is a golf club in Malaysia.

Tanah Merah Country Club is a prominent golfing destination on Singapore's east coast. The championship courses of the club are the Garden Course and the Tampines Course. The Garden Course has lush vegetation and intricate bunkering, while the Tampines Course has a links-style layout with wide fairways and challenging greens. Tanah Merah Country Club combines natural beauty with world-class facilities to create an unforgettable golfing experience.

Helpful Information

Most Singapore golf courses require golfers to hold a legitimate handicap. Visitors without a handicap can play if they arrange a round through certain tour operators or golf booking services. It is best to check with the golf courses to clarify the exact criteria and booking procedures.

Driving ranges, practice greens, and golf schools are standard features of Singapore golf courses for golfers looking to improve their game. Golf clubs and buggies are frequently available for rent at the courses.

Nature Reserves

Singapore is home to the Bukit Timah Nature Reserve.

Bukit Timah Nature Reserve is a green sanctuary in the heart of Singapore. Bukit Timah Hill, Singapore's tallest hill and one of the country's most significant portions of primary rainforest, is located here. Visitors can explore the reserve's extensive path system, which winds through dense forest and leads to the summit of Bukit Timah Hill. The reserve is famous among nature enthusiasts because it offers the opportunity to see a variety of plant and animal species, including the rare Raffles' Banded Langur.

Sungei Buloh Wetland Reserve is a Singapore wetlands reserve.

In Singapore's northern region, Sungei Buloh Wetland Reserve is a haven for migratory birds and a thriving ecosystem of mangroves, mudflats, and wetlands. The reserve has a network of boardwalks and trails, allowing visitors to explore the area's habitats and see wildlife. Birdwatchers can see a variety of species, including the beautiful migrating birds that visit the site during the migratory season. Sungei Buloh Wetland Reserve provides nature lovers and bird watchers with a serene and educational experience.

Labrador Nature Reserve

The Labrador Nature Reserve, in Singapore's southern region, is a coastal sanctuary combining natural beauty and historical value. Pathways wind through beautiful forests and lead to breathtaking views of the sea. Visitors can explore the area's rich biodiversity, including various plant and mammal species. The reserve is particularly well-known for its World War II antiquities, including the Labrador Battery and the Dragon's Teeth Gate, which add a historical layer to the natural experience.

The Wetlands of Chek Jawa

Chek Jawa Wetlands is a one-of-a-kind and ecologically diverse area on Pulau Ubin, an outlying island in northeastern Singapore. Wetlands with a mix of sandy beaches, mangroves, and seagrass lagoons are home to various marine and terrestrial animals. During low tide, tourists can walk along the boardwalks to explore the wetlands and see marine fauna such as seahorses, crabs, and sea stars. Chek Jawa Wetlands is a must-see for Singapore's marine biodiversity.

Helpful Information

To reduce the harm done to flora and wildlife, conserving the natural environment and following defined trails when visiting Singapore's nature reserves is critical. Visitors should also know the rules and regulations of each reserve's management authority, such as operating hours and restrictions on specific activities.

Various nature reserves offer guided tours and educational programs, allowing visitors to learn more about Singapore's ecosystems and conservation efforts. It would help if you visited each reserve's website or tourism office for information on guided tours and upcoming events.

CHAPTER EIGHTH

Shopping and entertainment
Shopping Malls
Orchard Avenue

Orchard Road is Singapore's premier retail district, surrounded by numerous malls offering diverse shopping options. The following are a few notable malls in the area:

ION Orchard: Located in the center of Orchard Road, ION Orchard is a refined shopping destination with worldwide designer labels, high-end retail outlets, and various restaurants.

Paragon: Located close to ION Orchard, Paragon is known for its upscale fashion and leisure establishments, such as designer labels, beauty stores, and gourmet food outlets.

Ngee Ann City: A well-known mall on Orchard Road, Ngee Ann City is a one-stop shopping destination with a mix of luxury brands, department stores, beauty salons, and a diverse selection of gourmet options.

Mandarin Gallery: Mandarin Gallery, located near the Mandarin Orchard Singapore Hotel, features a carefully curated selection of exceptional fashion, leisure, and cuisine shops.

These shopping centers typically open around 10:00 a.m. and shut at 10:00 p.m., while specific businesses and restaurants within the malls may have different hours of operation.

Marina Bay Sands
Marina Bay Sands is a fantastic integrated resort with a luxury hotel, a convention center, a casino, and a premier shopping mall. The Shoppes at Marina Bay Sands is a shopping paradise filled with high-end designer labels, luxury shops, and unique concept stores. Visitors can have a fantastic shopping experience while admiring the breathtaking views of Marina Bay. The mall opens at 10:30 a.m. until 11:00 p.m.

VivoCity
The HarbourFront waterfront is home to VivoCity, Singapore's largest shopping complex. It has a diverse retail mix, including worldwide fashion labels, technology stores, and lifestyle businesses. VivoCity also has many restaurants, a theater, and recreational facilities. The mall opens at 10:00 a.m. until ten o'clock p.m.

Changi Airport is a Work of Art
Jewel Changi Airport, located within Changi Airport, is a one-of-a-kind shopping and lifestyle destination. This architectural marvel is known for its magnificent indoor waterfall, lush gardens, and many retail and dining options. Visitors will find a mix of global brands, local shops, and specialty businesses. The Jewel Changi Airport opens from 10:00 a.m. to 10:00 p.m., with some restaurants staying open longer.

Bugis Street and Bugis Junction
Bugis Street and Bugis Junction are popular retail destinations in Singapore's cultural district. Bugis Street is well-known for its lively street market, where tourists may

get low-cost clothing, accessories, and gifts. Bugis Junction, located near Bugis Street, has a variety of retail companies, department stores, and dining options. These shopping malls typically open around 11:00 a.m. and shut down at 10:00 p.m.

Please remember that hours of operation and closing may vary during public holidays and festive seasons. For the most up-to-date information on operating hours, check the official website of the respective mall or contact their customer service.

Night Market
Chinatown Street Market
Trengganu Street, Pagoda Street, and Sago Street (Chinatown)
Chinatown Street Market is a well-known night market in Singapore's historic Chinatown neighborhood. The market has many stalls providing traditional Chinese goods, souvenirs, clothing, accessories, and handicrafts. Visitors can also sample local foods from adjacent food vendors and hawker hubs. Usually, the market opens at 6:00 p.m. and closes at 10:00 p.m. However, some vendors may begin setting up earlier in the day.

Geylang Serai (Malay Village).
The Geylang Serai Night Market comes alive during Ramadan, the Muslim holy month. It's in Geylang Serai, a cultural district known for its Malay and Muslim minorities. The market uniquely blends Malay cuisine, traditional costumes, vibrant decorations, and cultural performances. Visitors can browse a variety of vendors selling regional delicacies, clothing, accessories, and handicrafts. Typically, the market opens in the late afternoon and closes beyond midnight.

Clarke Quay Night Market
Located at Clarke Quay. On weekends and special events, Clarke Quay, a well-known riverside locale, offers a bustling night market. The market includes sellers selling clothing, accessories, artwork, and souvenirs. Visitors can enjoy the vibrant atmosphere, live entertainment, and multiple restaurants and cafes along the waterfront. The

market is open late afternoon to early evening and closes at 11:00 p.m.

The Locals' Night Market
Singapore has several locations.

The Local People Night Market is a mobile market that visits various locations in Singapore. It features local designers, artists, artisans, and small enterprises. Visitors can buy one-of-a-kind and handmade items such as apparel, art, and home decor, among other things. The market typically has live music, food stalls, and participatory activities. Opening and closing times may differ according to the specific venue and event. Thus, checking their official website or social media for information about upcoming markets is critical.

Night Markets in the Neighborhood (Pasar Malam)
Singapore's several neighborhoods
Pasar Malam, or "night market" in Malay, are ephemeral night markets in various Singapore residential zones. These markets sell multiple items, including clothing, accessories, home goods, toys, and street food. Pasar Malam has its distinct personality and local specialties. These markets' opening and closing times vary, but they often begin in the late afternoon and last until around 10:00 p.m.

Theaters and Shows
Esplanade Theatres on the Bay
1 Esplanade Drive, Singapore 038981 is the address.
The Esplanade - Theatres on the Bay is one of Singapore's most outstanding performing arts facilities in the Marina Bay neighborhood. Its unique architectural design, reminiscent of durian fruit, instantly recognizes it. The complex's venues include the Concert Hall, Theatre, Recital Studio, and Outdoor Theatre. The box office is typically open from 12:00 p.m. to 8:30 p.m., depending on the planned shows.

Victoria Theatre and Concert Hall
9 Empress Place, Singapore 179556 is the address.
The Victoria Theatre and Concert Hall, located along the Singapore River in the Civic District, is a historic venue that hosts a variety of cultural performances. Its two main venues are the Victoria Theatre and the Victoria Concert Hall. The opening timings may vary depending on the

booked shows. Visit the official website or contact the venue for the most up-to-date information.

Theatre at the Theatrical Centre
Level 3 of the National Library Building, 100 Victoria Street, Singapore 188064

The Drama Centre Theatre, located within the National Library Building in the Bugis neighborhood, serves as a venue for theatrical performances. The theater includes a proscenium stage and seating for 615 people. The scheduled performances usually determine the opening times. It is critical to check the theater's website or call the venue for specific show times.

Marina Bay Sands
Singapore 018956, 10 Bayfront Avenue.
Marina Bay Sands is a resort with various entertainment options, including world-class theater performances. The Sands Theatre at Marina Bay Sands features major international touring plays such as Broadway musicals and live concerts by well-known performers. Because show times vary according to the production, the most up-to-date information can be found on the official Marina Bay Sands website or by contacting the resort.
Cultural Exhibits

In addition to individual theaters, Singapore offers cultural activities that exhibit the country's rich history. These performances are sometimes given at cultural organizations or locations dedicated to preserving and showcasing varied ethnic practices. Traditional music, dance, and theater performances are frequently held at places like the Malay Heritage Centre, the Chinese Cultural Centre, and the Indian Heritage Centre. These performances' beginning and ending times may differ depending on the specific event and location.

CHAPTER NINE

Singaporean Cuisine
Local Delicacies

My first stop was at a bustling hawker center, where the sizzle of works and the rush and bustle of eager eaters created a vibrant scene. It is where I first tried the famous Hainanese Chicken Rice. The exquisite poached chicken, expertly mixed with aromatic rice and various wonderful flavors, astounded me. The dish's simplicity belied its incredible depth of flavor, and I couldn't stop ordering more.

As my culinary journey progressed, I was drawn to the fragrant seduction of Laksa. Smells of coconut milk, aromatic spices, and a symphony of seafood and fresh greens filled the air as steaming bowls of this spicy noodle soup lured me in. With each bite, I felt a scorching warmth wrap around my taste receptors, leaving me craving the next delicious mouthful.

The aroma of sizzling noodles drew my attention next, leading me to an establishment where Char Kway Teow was expertly prepared. The noodles dancing in the pan were a sight to behold, rich with smokey flavors and crammed with superb shrimp and excellent seasonings. The dish was a fantastic combination of textures and flavors, with the mild char adding an appealing touch that made it truly unique.

I entered a seafood paradise, eager to learn more, and discovered the famed Chili Crab. I found delicious meat encased in a tasty blend of spices, chilies, and acidic tomato sauce when I broke open the vivid red shells. The avalanche of flavors that resulted in my taste was spectacular. Every bite was a delight, a sweet and spicy symphony that played on my taste buds.

Looking for a change of pace, I entered an Indian restaurant where the enticing aroma of freshly cooked Roti Prata filled the air. Watching the cook's skilled hands stretch and shape the dough into a flaky and crispy treat. When paired with a savory curry dipping sauce, each mouthful of buttery bread was a delightful explosion of sensations, delivering a sense of comfort and warmth.

In the morning, I found the simple yet delicious pleasure of Kaya Toast. The crunchy toast, topped with aromatic coconut jam and butter, created a flavor symphony that made me smile. I CONNECTED TO SINGAPORE'S RICH HERITAGE AND THE STORIES WOVEN INTO ITS CULINARY TAPESTRY when I ate this exquisite delicacy alongside a cup of aromatic kopi at a typical kopitiam.

As my journey across Singapore's traditional delicacies ended, I realized each dish had told me a unique story. From street food vendors to premium eateries, every flavor offered a glimpse into Singapore's rich ethnic tapestry. The experiences had awakened my senses, broadened my culinary horizons, and left an indelible imprint on my mouth and heart.

So, if you find yourself in Singapore's distinct city-state, follow your taste buds on a culinary adventure. Learn about the regional delicacies and the history behind each dish, and allow the flavors to transport you to a world of gourmet delight.

Hainanese Chicken Rice

Hainanese Chicken Rice is a popular Singaporean dish that has gained international acclaim. Poached chicken is served with aromatic rice cooked in chicken broth and seasoned with chili sauce, ginger paste, and dark soy sauce. The result is a delectable combination of flavors and textures that will leave you wanting more. This delicious delicacy is available at hawker centers, food courts, and specialty chicken rice outlets all across the island.

Laksa

Laksa is a hot noodle soup with Chinese and Malay flavors popular in Malaysia. Thick rice noodles are drowned in a delicious coconut-based curry broth and garnished with shrimp, fish cake, tofu puffs, and bean sprouts. The coconut milk's richness, the curry's spiciness, and the aroma of herbs and spices all work together to create a unique and exquisite flavor. Katong Laksa, a type of Laksa, is a local favorite with particular characteristics.

Char Kway Teow

Char Kway Teow is a stir-fried noodle dish that exemplifies Singapore's fondness for wok hei, or the smoky scent of high-heat cooking. Flat rice noodles are stir-fried with shrimp, Chinese sausage, bean sprouts, and eggs in a savory soy sauce, chili paste, and other seasonings. The result is a delicious, slightly blackened dish that delivers a punch. Look for hawkers or street food sellers who specialize in this popular delicacy.

Chili with Crab
Chili Crab is a Singaporean seafood specialty with international acclaim. Mud crabs are stir-fried with chile, ginger, garlic, and soy sauce in a sour and spicy tomato-based sauce. The sauce is a beautiful blend of sweetness and spice that complements the soft and delicious crab flesh. To make this messy yet exquisite dish, crack open the shells and devour the rich flavors with mantou, a steamed bun.

Roti Prata
Roti Prata, a popular Indian-influenced food, is a flaky, crispy flatbread served with curry. The dough is stretched, twisted, and fried on a griddle to achieve a wonderful texture. It can be eaten alone or with additional ingredients like egg, cheese, or even banana for a sweet twist. In Singapore's Indian restaurants and hawker areas, Roti Prata is a popular breakfast and supper alternative.

Kaya Toast
Kaya Toast is a popular Singaporean morning item. It's made with toasted bread, kaya, a sweet and fragrant coconut jam, and a slab of butter. Combining crispy bread, creamy butter, and fragrant kaya creates a soothing and delectable bite. Complement it with a cup of kopi, or local-style coffee or tea, for a truly authentic experience. Traditional coffee shops called kopitiams are popular places to indulge in this simple yet delightful pleasure.

Hawker Centers and Food Courts
Experiments in Traditional Culinary
Peranakan Cuisine
One of Singapore's most memorable traditional dining experiences is Peranakan, Straits Chinese, or Nyonya cuisine. Peranakan cuisine blends ingredients from China, Malaysia, and Indonesia to create a harmonious blend of spicy, sweet, and sour flavors. Traditional Peranakan dishes include Ayam Buah Keluak (black nut chicken), Babi Pongteh (braised pork in fermented soybean paste), and Nyonya Laksa (spicy coconut milk noodle soup). Dine at historical venues such as Violet Oon Singapore or The Blue Ginger to understand this distinct culinary tradition.

Hawker Centers
Every trip to Singapore is complete with experiencing the vibrant atmosphere of the city-state's hawker centers. Locals and visitors alike go to these rich open-air food courts for low-cost traditional meals. Many popular hawker centers are Maxwell Food Centre, Chinatown Complex Food Centre, and Tiong Bahru Market. Hawker centers serve various cuisines, including the famed Hainanese Chicken Rice, Char Kway Teow, Roti Prata, and Satay. They are the ideal place to sample a variety of distinctive Singaporean dishes.

Katong Laksa
Katong Laksa is a traditional Peranakan dish that originated in the Katong neighborhood. Thick rice noodles are served in a creamy, fragrant coconut-based curry broth, topped with shrimp, fish cake, and laksa leaves. Unlike other types

of Laksa, Katong Laksa comes with pre-cut noodles, making it easier to taste. Go to Katong or Joo Chiat Road to find vendors specializing in this popular and delectable dish.

Satay
Satay is a popular Singaporean street food that is similar to Malay cuisine. Skewers of marinated and grilled meat, typically chicken or beef, are served with cucumber, onion slices, and a tangy peanut sauce. The aroma of the charred flesh and the nutty flavors of the spice complement each other beautifully. Satay Street in Lau Pa Sat in the evenings offers a whole Satay experience, with vendors lining the street tempting you with their sizzling skewers.

Typical Breakfasts
To fully immerse yourself in Singapore's gastronomic culture, begin your day with a typical breakfast. Visit a nearby kopitiam (coffee shop) and enjoy a buffet including Kaya Toast, soft-boiled eggs, and a cup of aromatic kopi or teh. The Kaya Toast combines toasted bread with coconut jam and a generous slab of butter to create the ideal balance of sweetness and richness. Dip the toast into the runny eggs seasoned with soy sauce and pepper for a delightful and realistic morning experience.

Halal And Vegetarian Options
Halal Foods
Arab Street and Kampong Glam
Arab Street and Kampong Glam are well-known for their extensive selections of Middle Eastern and Arab restaurants. There's a wide range of halal goodies,

including hearty plates of chicken biryani and exquisite kebabs, aromatic falafel wraps, and fantastic shawarma. Go to Zam Zam Restaurant or Beirut Grill for a truly authentic Middle Eastern experience.

Geylang Serai

Geylang Serai is a thriving district known for its distinct Malay and Indonesian food culture. You'll discover a large assortment of halal-certified vendors and restaurants providing a variety of cuisines here. Traditional Malay dishes include:

Nasi Lemak (fragrant coconut rice with a variety of accompaniments).

Mee Rebus (yellow noodles in a rich, spicy broth).

Roti John (a baguette filled with minced pork and onions).

The Geylang Serai Bazaar comes alive with halal street food vendors during Ramadan.

Hawker Centers

Singapore's hawker centers have an abundance of halal options. These lively food courts are teeming with stalls serving a variety of cuisines, including Chinese, Malay, Indian, and others. Look for halal-certified booths to enjoy popular dishes like Hainanese Chicken Rice, Mee Goreng (spicy fried noodles), and Satay. The halal stalls of Adam Road Food Centre and Pasir Ris Central Hawker Centre are well-known.

Vegetarian Foods

Miniature India

Little India is a bustling area with plenty of vegetarian options. Explore the vibrant streets and sample vegetarian versions of typical Indian dishes like dosas (fermented crepes), paneer tikka (grilled cheese cubes), and vegetable biryani. Komala Vilas and Ananda Bhavan are two popular options for traditional South Indian vegetarian meals.

Orchard Road and the CBD

Vegetarian-friendly restaurants may be found even in the busiest retail districts of Orchard Road and the Central Business District (CBD). Numerous options are available, ranging from global vegetarian businesses to elegant eateries. Original Sin, a Mediterranean-inspired vegetarian restaurant known for its odd vegetarian dishes, or Real Food, known for its organic and nutritious options, serves a packed **Plant-Based Lunch**

Cafes that support a healthy way of life

Singapore has seen an upsurge in health-conscious cafes and eateries catering to vegetarian and vegan diets. These restaurants focus on fresh, plant-based ingredients to create different food that is both delicious and nutritious. Look for cafes like Afterglow by Anglow that provide healthy bowls, raw vegan snacks, and cold-pressed juices.

Popular Restaurants Locations

Burnt Tips

20 Teck Lim Road, Singapore 088391
Entry time: 11:45 a.m.
Closing times: 2:00 p.m. (Lunch), 6:00 p.m. (Dinner).
Odette

National Gallery Singapore

1 St Andrew's Road, #01-04, Singapore 178957.
Hours of operation: noon.
Closing times: 1:30 p.m. (Lunch), 7:00 p.m. (Dinner).
Din Tai Fung (many locations)
Singapore locations include Ion Orchard, Paragon, and **Marina Bay Sands**

Hours of operation: 11:00 a.m.
At 9:00 p.m., the store closed.

Jumbo Seafood (Dempsey Hill)
#01-16 11 Dempsey Road, Singapore 249673
Hours of operation: noon.
3:00 p.m. 5:30 p.m. (Dinner).

Swee Choon Tim Sum Restaurant
Singapore: 183-191 Jalan Besar, 208882.
Hours of operation: 11:00 a.m. 6:00 p.m. (Friday-Sunday). (Monday-Thursday).
Time to close: 2:30 p.m. 2:00 a.m. (Friday-Sunday). (Monday-Thursday).

Candlenut
17A Dempsey Road, Singapore 249676.
Hours of operation: noon.
Closing times: 2:30 p.m. (Lunch), 6:00 p.m. (Dinner).

Wild Honey (many locations)
Scotts Square and the Mandarin Gallery are two stores in Singapore.
Hours of operation: 9:00 a.m.
Closing time: 10:30 p.m.

Tiong Bahru Bakery on Eng Hoon Street
56 Eng Hoon Street, #01-70, Singapore 160056
Hours of operation: 8:00 a.m.
Closing time: 8:00 p.m.

Haji Lane (Multiple Restaurants)
Haji Lane in Singapore's Kampong Glam
Many businesses in the area have different opening and closing times.

Please remember that opening and closing times may vary, so always check the official website or contact the restaurant before visiting for the most up-to-date information.

CHAPTER TEN

Transportation in Singapore
MRT Stands for Mass Rapid Transit

Singapore's Mass Rapid Transit (MRT) system is a modern and efficient public transportation system that gives residents and visitors speedy and dependable travel alternatives. The MRT is the backbone of Singapore's transportation infrastructure, connecting a range of towns, economic sectors, and tourist destinations throughout the island. The MRT is a popular choice for commuting and exploring the city-state due to its extensive coverage, frequent train runs, and user-friendly facilities. Let's look at Singapore's MRT system's key characteristics and benefits.

Connectivity and Network

Singapore's MRT network comprises multiple lines that traverse the entire island. According to my knowledge, the MRT system has five main lines that will terminate in September 2021: the East-West Line (EWL), the North-South Line (NSL), the North-East Line (NEL), the Circle Line (CCL), and the Downtown Line (DTL). These lines connect at crucial interchange stations, providing convenient transfers between routes. In addition, the Thomson-East Coast Line (TEL) and Jurong Region Line (JRL) are now under development to improve connection.

Hours of operation and frequency

The MRT runs from early morning until late night, providing continuous daily service. Trains usually begin running around 5:30 a.m. and operate until after midnight.

However, it's worth emphasizing that the precise working hours for each line and station may vary significantly. Contact the official SMRT (Singapore Mass Rapid Transit) website for the most up-to-date information, or refer to station signage.

Trains operate at higher frequencies during peak hours, typically from 7:00 a.m. to 9:00 a.m. and 5:00 p.m. to 8:00 p.m. on weekdays, to satisfy increasing passenger demand. Outside of peak hours, trains run at regular intervals, frequently ranging from 3 to 8 minutes, ensuring that commuters have as little downtime as possible.

System of Ticketing and Fares

Passengers can use the EZ-Link card or the Singapore Tourist Pass to gain access to the MRT system. The EZ-Link card is a contactless smart card that can be loaded with saved money and used to pay for fares across numerous public transportation, including the MRT, buses, and select taxis. The Singapore Tourist Pass, which can be purchased at selected MRT stations, offers unrestricted travel for a predetermined length of time (1, 2, or 3 days) and is an ideal alternative for travelers.

MRT fares are distance-based, which implies that the distance decides the fare traveled. The fare structure is meant to be inexpensive, with savings available for off-peak travel, concession cardholders, and regular commuters. The EZ-Link card or contactless payment systems are utilized at MRT stations to enable a smooth and rapid entry and exit process.

Amenities and Accessibility

Singapore's MRT system is designed to accommodate all passengers, including those with mobility difficulties. Most MRT stations offer elevators, escalators, and barrier-free services to ensure that everyone has easy access. Every train includes priority seating for older citizens, pregnant women, and those with impairments, fostering inclusivity and comfort throughout transit.

MRT stations also provide a variety of amenities to improve the passenger experience. These include train arrival time information boards, platform screen doors for additional security, public restrooms, convenience stores, and food and beverage outlets. Some stations even have bright artwork and displays, transforming the MRT experience into a cultural-historical museum of Singapore.

Buses

SBS Transit and SMRT Buses are the two leading bus companies in Singapore. These businesses run a comprehensive network of bus lines serving residential and commercial regions. The bus routes cross the entire island, making practically every section of Singapore accessible by bus.

Route Network in Depth

Singapore's bus system has a broad route network connecting various city regions. The routes are intended to give simple coverage of residential neighborhoods, business centers, and key tourist destinations. Whether you want to explore the busy streets of Chinatown, shop on

Orchard Road, or view cultural icons, there's sure to be a bus route that can get you there.

Service Frequency and Timeliness

Buses in Singapore run on a regular and predictable timetable, ensuring that passengers have little time to wait. During peak hours, buses generally run at 5 to 10-minute intervals, allowing for efficient transportation during busy periods. Outside peak hours, the frequency may vary substantially, but buses keep a regular schedule to fulfill passenger demand.

Information and Technology in Real Time

Singapore's buses are outfitted with cutting-edge technology and real-time information systems to improve the passenger experience. Electronic display boards at bus terminals provide real-time information on bus arrival timetables, allowing passengers to plan their journeys better. Furthermore, smartphone apps and web platforms offer real-time updates on bus routes, schedules, and disruptions, ensuring passengers have the most up-to-date information.

Amenities and Accessibility

Singapore's buses are designed to accommodate all passengers, including those with mobility difficulties. Low-floor buses with ramps are employed on most routes, allowing wheelchair users, older people, and families with strollers easy boarding and alighting. Every bus provides priority seats for needy people, fostering diversity and comfort throughout transit.

Interchanges for Buses and Integrated Transit Hubs

Singapore has created several bus interchanges and integrated transportation hubs to promote seamless transfers between buses and other forms of transportation. These interchanges, which include Toa Payoh Interchange, Jurong East Interchange, and Serangoon Interchange, serve as crucial transit hubs where multiple bus routes converge. They are also linked to MRT stations, allowing consumers to quickly changeover between bus and train services.

Payment Options and Affordability

Taking the bus in Singapore is a cost-effective choice for both residents and visitors. Similar to the MRT system, the fare structure is distance-based, guaranteeing that passengers pay a reasonable fare based on the distance traveled. Bus fares can be paid with the EZ-Link card, which is also used for the MRT and other modes of public transportation. Cash is also accepted, although tourists are encouraged to use contactless payment alternatives for faster and more convenient transactions.

Taxis and Ride-sharing Companies

In addition to the MRT system and buses, Singapore provides a variety of taxi and ride-sharing services to fulfill the mobility demands of residents and visitors. Taxis offer convenient, comfortable door-to-door service, and ride-sharing services offer economical and on-demand transportation. Let us review the essential characteristics and benefits of taxis and ride-sharing services in Singapore.

Singapore Taxis

Taxis are frequently available in Singapore and provide a trustworthy form of transportation. Here is some crucial taxi information to know:

Taxi Types: Singapore has multiple taxi firms, each with its fleet. ComfortDelGro Taxis (blue), SMRT Taxis (yellow), and TransCab Taxis (white) are the most common. To guarantee passenger safety, all cabs are licensed and supervised.

Taxis can be waved down by raising your hand or at designated taxi stands near large institutions, retail malls, and transportation hubs. The "Taxi" sign on the roof signals the taxi's availability.

Metered Fare: Taxis in Singapore charge a metered fare. The tariff is computed depending on the distance traveled and the time spent, with additional surcharges imposed during peak hours, late nights, and for specialized sites such as the airport. It is crucial to remember that electronic road pricing (ERP) charges may apply during peak hours and will be used on the ticket.

Taxi Booking: Taxis can be pre-booked utilizing phone apps, online platforms, or by calling taxi firms directly. Reservations are essential during peak hours or while traveling to specified areas.

Air conditioning, comfortable seating, and skilled drivers versed in the city's streets are regular features of Singapore taxis. Taxis also have plenty of storage capacity, making them suitable for bag passengers.

Singapore Ride-sharing Services

Ride-sharing services have risen in popularity in Singapore, giving an alternate and convenient means of transportation. Grab is Singapore's most well-known ride-sharing service. Everything you need to know about ride-sharing services is right here:

Booking a Ride: Ride-sharing services can be accessed using smartphone apps. Download the app, establish an account, and book a ride by indicating your pick-up and drop-off spots. The app will provide information on the driver, an expected arrival time, and the cost.

Pricing & Payment: In Singapore, ride-sharing services give upfront pricing, permitting you to see the projected fare before finishing the booking. Payment is made electronically via the app, often linked to a credit card or other digital payment alternatives.

Vehicle Alternatives: Ride-sharing services offer a variety of vehicle options to fulfill a variety of purposes. Examples are regular cars, larger vehicles for groups or families, and luxury vehicles for a more joyful experience.

Ride-sharing businesses prioritize passenger safety by conducting background checks on drivers and adding safety measures into the app, such as sharing ride data with friends or family members and providing an emergency assistance button.

Other Firms: Ride-sharing companies frequently provide additional services such as food delivery and courier services, increasing their convenience beyond passenger transportation.

Renting a Car or a Bicycle
Renting a Car
Rental Agencies: Several car rental agencies, both foreign and domestic, operate in Singapore. Avis, Budget, Hertz, and other major firms are represented. These firms have several pick-up sites, including the airport and the city center, making acquiring and returning the rental car easier.

Driving License: To rent a car in Singapore, you must have a valid driving license from your home country or an international driving permit (IDP). Check the rental agency's specific policies to verify compliance.

Booking & Reservation: You should reserve your rental car ahead of time, especially during peak tourist seasons. Online booking tools or direct contact with rental firms may ensure excellent rates and availability.

Rental organizations commonly mandate a minimum age for drivers, usually 21 years or older, with at least one year of driving experience. To cover any potential damages or additional charges, a refundable deposit or credit card authorization is usually asked at the time of rental.

Insurance & Coverage: In Singapore, comprehensive insurance generally covers rental cars. However, checking the policy specifics and looking into other insurance options for more protection is vital.

Renting a Bicycle
Bicycle Rental Shops: Various rental shops in Singapore sell bicycles for short-term use. These companies are generally located near parks, tourist attractions, or

designated bike routes. East Coast Park, Marina Bay, and Sentosa Island are famous tourist destinations.

Bicycle rental costs vary depending on the period and type of bicycle rented. Hourly and daily rental alternatives are available, allowing you to decide the rental duration that best meets your needs. Rental costs usually include a refundable deposit.

Bicycle rental businesses feature safety goods such as helmets and bicycle locks. These devices are indicated for your protection and to avoid theft.

Bicycle Infrastructure: Singapore boasts an extensive network of bicycle pathways and dedicated lanes, making cycling across the city safe and pleasurable. To guarantee a smooth and safe cycling excursion, familiarize yourself with the riding rules and regulations.

Bike-sharing firms: Besides rental shops, bike-sharing companies such as oBike and SG Bike rent dockless bicycles via smartphone apps. These services give convenience in terms of pick-up and drop-off locations.

Routes for Walking and Cycling
Walking Paths

Singapore River Promenade: The Singapore River Promenade is a lovely strolling promenade along the Singapore River's banks. This walk from Robertson Quay to Marina Bay carries you past historical attractions, modern structures, and unique dining and entertainment alternatives.

The Southern Ridges is a network of walking pathways that connect several parks and nature reserves in Singapore's southern region. This picturesque stroll offers stunning panoramas, lush foliage, and the chance to encounter native flora and wildlife. The highlights are Henderson Waves, a pedestrian bridge with a remarkable architecture, and Mount Faber's treetop hike.

Gardens by the Bay: Stroll around the iconic Gardens by the Bay's well-designed strolling trails. Wander through the Supertree Grove, walk along the OCBC Skyway, and visit the several themed gardens, such as the Flower Dome and Cloud Forest. The Gardens by the Bay offer a one-of-a-kind horticultural experience amid the metropolis.

MacRitchie Reservoir Park: MacRitchie Reservoir Park provides a tranquil walking track surrounded by nature. The TreeTop Walk, a suspension bridge with panoramic views of the surrounding forest canopy, is a highlight of the park. The park also has scenic pathways that wind around the reservoir, providing a calm escape from the rush and bustle of the city.

Cycle Routes

East Coast Park: East Coast Park is home to one of Singapore's most famous bicycle routes. This magnificent coastal park spans 15 kilometers and has dedicated bike lanes, seaside vistas, and services such as food outlets, BBQ pits, and water sports facilities.

Park Connector Network (PCN): The Park Connector Network (PCN) in Singapore is a comprehensive network of bike lanes that connect parks, neighborhoods, and key attractions throughout the island. The PCN provides a secure and enjoyable riding experience, allowing you to explore different areas of Singapore at your leisure.

Pulau Ubin: Take a ferry to Pulau Ubin, a rural Singaporean island, and explore its bike paths. With its traditional kampong (village) environment, breathtaking landscape, and pristine nature, the island promises a one-of-a-kind riding experience. Rent a bicycle and enjoy the island's rustic charm.

Marina Bay Sands to East Coast Park: This bike path connects the famed Marina Bay Sands neighborhood to the lovely East Coast Park. Enjoy fantastic city skyline views while riding along the waterfront promenade and enjoying the lively ambiance of East Coast Park's recreational services and dining selections.

Tips and Safety

When cycling on roads or shared routes, respect traffic rules and signals.

When cycling, utilize adequate safety equipment, such as helmets.

Keep yourself hydrated and sun-protected.

Be wary of pedestrians and yield when necessary.

Before engaging in outdoor activities, check the weather forecast and avoid cycling during severe rain or storms.

CHAPTER ELEVEN

Accommodation Options
Resorts and Hotels

Fragrance Hotel - Bugis
Fragrance Hotel: Bugis, strategically located in the Middle of the city, offers pleasant and cheap rooms with modern comforts. Its handy location enables easy access to renowned attractions such as Bugis Street Market and Haji Lane, making it a good alternative for budget-conscious tourists.

Ibis Singapore on Bencoolen
The Ibis, Singapore on Bencoolen, offers pleasant and well-equipped rooms at a reasonable price. Guests may quickly explore Singapore's major shopping and entertainment districts because of the hotel's proximity to Orchard Road and the Marina Bay region.

Hotel Boss
Hotel Boss, located near Lavender MRT station, provides economical hotel options with clean and comfortable rooms. Its good position offers you quick access to several attractions, such as Gardens by the Bay and Marina Bay Sands.

Santa Grand Hotel East Coast
Santa Grand Hotel East Coast, located in the bustling East Coast region, offers cheap rooms with a warm atmosphere. The hotel's proximity to East Coast Park and its superb seafood restaurants, make it a popular choice for budget travelers searching for a quiet coastal vacation.

The Pod Boutique Capsule Hotel
The Pod Boutique Capsule Hotel offers cheap capsule-style lodging without sacrificing comfort for budget guests looking for a unique experience. It is perfectly positioned in the heritage-rich Arab Street district, allowing easy access to cultural landmarks such as Sultan Mosque and Malay **Heritage Centre**
Hotel 81 - Rochor:
Hotel 81 - Rochor: provides cheap rooms with minimal amenities in a handy location near the Rochor MRT station. Its proximity to Little India and the Mustafa Centre makes it a good alternative for those interested in experiencing Singapore's ethnic variety.
Fragrance Hotel - Imperial
Fragrance Hotel: Imperial, located in the busy Geylang district, offers inexpensive rooms and quick access to local eateries and cultural sites. Its proximity to the Aljunied MRT station allows guests to explore various city sections quickly. **Venue Hotel**
Venue Hotel in the Joo Chiat district features affordable rooms with modern décor. Because of its proximity to heritage shophouses, elegant cafés, and local gourmet alternatives, the hotel is a good choice for budget travelers seeking an authentic Singapore experience.
Hotel Yan
Hotel Yan, located in the culturally rich Balestier district, provides cheap rooms with a modern flair. The hotel's proximity to prominent monuments, such as the Sun Yat

Sen Nanyang Memorial Hall and the Whampoa Food Centre, suits guests interested in history and local food.

Aqueen Hotel Paya Lebar
Aqueen Hotel Paya Lebar offers low-cost rooms with sleek and modern decor. Its proximity to the Paya Lebar MRT station allows easy access to critical locations such as the bustling Geylang Serai market and the Paya Lebar Quarter.

Budget Accommodation
Adler Hostel
In the lively Chinatown neighborhood, Adler Hostel offers inexpensive dormitory-style rooms and private capsules. The hostel's modern decor, sumptuous bedding, and inviting atmosphere make it a popular choice for budget travelers.

MET A Space Pod
With its space-themed pods, MET A Space Pod gives a one-of-a-kind hotel experience. This budget-friendly hostel in the famous Boat Quay district offers contemporary pods built with modern comforts for a comfortable stay.

Capsule Pod Boutique Hostel
Capsule Pod Boutique Hostel, ideally located near Arab Street and Haji Lane, offers cheap capsule-style beds with privacy curtains. The hostel also has public rooms, a rooftop garden, and a beautiful lounge room for mingling.

Footprints Hostel
Footprints Hostel, located in Little India, provides economical lodging in a vibrant and culturally diverse atmosphere. The hostel offers clean and comfortable

dormitory accommodations, a community kitchen, and a welcoming atmosphere.

5footway.inn Project Bugis
5footway.inn Project Bugis, located near the Bugis MRT station, provides economic individual and dormitory accommodations. It delivers a unique and economical overnight experience with its heritage shophouse setting and near attractions such as Arab Street and Kampong Glam.

The Pod at Beach Road Boutique Capsule Hotel
The Pod at Beach Road Boutique Capsule Hotel provides cheap capsule-style lodgings near Bugis and Kampong Glam. Its modern structure, small pods, and handy location make it a fantastic alternative for budget-conscious tourists.

Mitraa Inn
Mitraa Inn is a low-cost guesthouse in the lively Little India district. It offers clean and attractive dormitory-style rooms and common areas for socialization. The hostel's proximity to Little India's bustling marketplaces and eateries adds to its attractiveness.

Beds and Dreams Inn at Chinatown
Beds and Dreams Inn, located in the core of Chinatown, provides economical lodging with a lovely and welcoming ambiance. The hostel offers dormitories and private apartments, making it perfect for lone travelers and groups.

The Bohemian Chic Hostel
The Bohemian Chic Hostel in Lavender offers an inexpensive dormitory and individual rooms in a charming and artistic atmosphere. The hostel's social rooms, which

include a rooftop patio and a cozy lounge, are great for meeting other guests.

Atlantis Pods at Little India
Atlantis Pods, located in the lively Little India district, offers cheap capsule-style rooms. The pods have cozy beds and personal conveniences, making for a pleasant and economical stay in a vibrant neighborhood.

These cheap Singapore hotels give guests comfortable and economical options, allowing them to enjoy the city without breaking the bank.

Serviced Apartment
Orchard Scotts Residences
Orchard Scotts Residences on the iconic Orchard Road offers excellent serviced apartments with attractive designs and modern conveniences. Residents can enjoy the site's stunning gardens, swimming pools, and recreational facilities.

Ascott Raffles Place Singapore
Ascott Raffles Place Singapore, located in the heart of the Central Business District, offers extensive and well-appointed serviced apartments. The facility includes several services, including a fitness center, a business center, and complimentary breakfast.

Fraser Residence Orchard, Singapore
In the iconic Orchard Road shopping hub, Fraser Residence Orchard offers exquisite serviced apartments. The apartments include modern design, fully equipped kitchens, and access to amenities like a gym, swimming pool, and rooftop terrace.

Pan Pacific Serviced Suites Orchard, Singapore
The Pan Pacific Serviced Suites Orchard provides excellent serviced apartments with breathtaking views of the metropolitan cityscape. The property, located on the famous Orchard Road, offers easy access to shopping, dining, and entertainment opportunities.

Capri by Fraser, Changi City / Singapore
Capri by Fraser is a contemporary serviced apartment near Changi Business Park and the Singapore Expo. The hotel includes beautifully-designed flats and services such as a 24-hour gym, an outdoor pool, and complimentary high-speed internet access.

Somerset Bencoolen Singapore
Somerset Bencoolen Singapore, located in the heart of Bencoolen Street, provides extensive and completely furnished serviced flats. A gymnasium, a residents' club, and a rooftop swimming pool are among the amenities accessible at the property.

Citadines Mount Sophia Singapore
Citadines Mount Sophia is a serviced apartment in the popular Bras Basah-Bugis neighborhood. The resort includes comfortable apartments with well-equipped kitchens and amenities such as a fitness center and rooftop swimming pool.

Oakwood Premier AMTD Singapore
In the heart of Singapore's Central Business District, Oakwood Premier AMTD Singapore offers magnificent serviced apartments. The apartments include contemporary

design, fully equipped kitchens, and access to amenities such as a fitness center and swimming pool.

Far East Plaza Residences

Far East Plaza Residences provides serviced flats in Singapore's iconic Orchard Road district. The apartments are big and well-appointed, and occupants can access amenities such as a swimming pool, gym, and sauna.

Village Residence Robertson Quay

Village Residence Robertson Quay offers serviced apartments with modern decor near the magnificent Singapore River. The hotel offers various services, such as a gym, an outdoor pool, and grilling facilities.

These Singapore-serviced apartments offer a comfortable and convenient stay experience for both short and long-term guests, blending home comforts with hotel-like amenities and conveniences.

Guesthouses and Hostels

The InnCrowd Backpackers' Hostel

The InnCrowd Backpackers' Hostel, located in the vibrant Little India neighborhood, provides economical dormitory-style accommodation in a pleasant and communal setting. The hostel features social areas, a rooftop garden, and regularly organized events for guests.

Beary Best Hostel

Beary Best is located in the Chinatown neighborhood. The hostel provides warm and cheap dormitory rooms with excellent beds. The hostel features a community lounge, a fully equipped kitchen, and a rooftop terrace where guests may relax and interact.

Adler Hostel
Adler Hostel, located in Chinatown's center, features private and dormitory-style accommodations. The hostel provides modern decor, comfy mattresses, and social areas where guests may relax and meet other travelers.

Backpackers' Inn Chinatown
Backpackers' Inn Chinatown offers affordable dormitory-style lodging in a prime location near the Chinatown MRT station. The hostel provides modest amenities, a communal kitchen, and a warm ambiance, making it a popular alternative for budget-conscious travelers.

The Shophouse Hostel
The Shophouse Hostel, located in the prominent Arab Street neighborhood, offers budget-friendly dormitory rooms with a unique and pleasant ambiance. The hostel has a community lounge, shared kitchen, and rooftop terrace for visitors' enjoyment.

Five Stones Hostel
Five Stones Hostel, located in the historic Arab Street district, provides comfortable and cheap dormitory rooms with individual lockers. The hostel has a public space, a fully equipped kitchen, and a courtyard where guests can relax.

Bunc Hostel
Bunc Hostel in the bustling Little India neighborhood provides modern and cheap dormitory-style rooms. The hostel has a community lounge, a rooftop patio, and a variety of events and activities for guests to participate in.

Fisher BnB:
Fisher BnB, located in the Joo Chiat district, provides affordable individual and dormitory-style lodgings with a comfortable and welcoming ambiance. The guesthouse offers a shared kitchen, a garden, and a patio where guests can rest.

Meadows Hostel
Meadows Hostel is adjacent to the Lavender MRT station and offers affordable dormitory-style rooms with limited amenities. The hostel has a community lounge, a shared kitchen, and a rooftop garden for visitors to rest and speak.

Dream Lodge
Dream Lodge, located in the Bugis neighborhood, provides cheap dormitory-style rooms with comfortable bunk beds. The hostel features a shared space, a fully equipped kitchen, and a rooftop patio with fantastic city views.

These Singapore hostels and guesthouses offer economical living options for budget tourists and a variety of amenities and public locations that foster a friendly and inviting environment. They are great for travelers looking for a low-cost stay and the possibility to meet other explorers from around the world.

Twelve Chapter

Cultural Etiquette and Tips
Multiculturalism and Respect:

Singaporeans are immensely proud of their cosmopolitan culture, and cultural appreciation is profoundly embedded in their ideas. When visiting Singapore, it is crucial to appreciate and respect the city-state's diversity. Respect for different ethnic customs, beliefs, and behaviors is vital for establishing unity and mutual understanding.

Salutations and Motions:

Greetings in Singapore differ according to ethnic origin. While it is common to shake hands, waiting for a local to initiate the ritual is usually advisable. Salam is a Malay and Indian greeting that consists of a quick right-hand shake with the left hand on the heart. It is traditional to bow when approaching seniors or those of higher social standing.

Language and Communication:

Singapore is a multilingual country with English as its primary language. On the other hand, understanding a few simple phrases in Mandarin, Malay, or Tamil may be helpful. Because Singaporeans appreciate civility and harmony in their interactions, it is vital to adopt a respectful tone and abstain from overly harsh language when chatting.

Dining Etiquette:

Food and dining etiquette are hugely significant in Singaporean culture. When invited to someone's home or dining out, waiting for the host to begin eating before you start is customary. Singaporeans favor chopsticks.

However, forks and spoons are also commonly used. Arranging chopsticks vertically in a rice dish resembles how incense sticks are used at funerals. It is common to sample everything on the table and applaud the food.

Gift Giving and Receiving:
Bringing a small gift for the host when visiting a Singaporean home is common. To show respect, presents should be given and accepted with both hands. Fruit baskets, chocolates, and souvenirs from your native country are all fantastic presents. Local culture considers sharp tools and white flowers unpleasant and should be avoided.

Religious Sensitivity:
Singapore's diverse religious community includes Buddhists, Muslims, Hindus, and Christians. When visiting sacred locations, dress modestly and respect any specified regulations or procedures. It is also necessary to follow religious practices like taking off one's shoes, covering one's head, and avoiding touching holy artifacts unless expressly permitted.

Greetings & Customs
Dress Code
Casual Attire:
Singaporeans prefer to dress informally, especially in everyday situations. The tropical environment favors the wearing of a light, airy clothing. Inhabitants often wear T-shirts, shorts, sundresses, and skirts. However, modesty is still prized in Singaporean culture. Therefore, incredibly exposing or provocative apparel may be regarded as improper.

Business Attire:
Singaporeans frequently dress professionally in professional environments. Female business wear consists of formal dresses, pantsuits, or skirts paired with blouses, whereas male business attire consists of tailored suits, dress shirts, and ties. Dress conservatively and modestly, and avoid flashy or expensive apparel. The dress code may fluctuate slightly depending on the occupation, with more relaxed wear encouraged in creative sectors.

Religious Sites and Ceremonies:
Because Singapore is home to many religious sects, it is vital to dress correctly when visiting sacred sites or attending festivities. Modest clothing that covers the shoulders, knees, and occasionally even the head is expected in places of worship. Sarongs and wraps are frequently available at the entry for anyone who needs to cover up. Slip-on shoes are helpful because shoes must be removed before approaching certain religious places.

Social Events and Nightlife:
Singapore features a lively social scene as well as a busy nightlife. Singaporeans wish to look fashionable when attending social events such as cocktail parties, nightclubs, or fine restaurants. Men often wear tailored shirts, trousers, jeans, and eye-catching footwear. Women should wear cocktail dresses, cute shirts with skirts or pants, appropriate jewelry, and heels. The venue's specific dress code or standards, on the other hand, must be followed.

Culture Festivals & Celebrations:

Singaporeans celebrate many cultural festivals throughout the year, including Chinese New Year, Deepavali, Hari Raya, and Christmas. During these significant festivities, individuals frequently dress in traditional costumes. Women may wear cheongsams (Chinese costumes) during Chinese New Year, sarees during Deepavali, or baju kurung during Hari Raya. Adopting the occasion's traditional costume not only shows respect but also adds to the festive ambiance of the celebrations.

Beachwear and Recreation:
Singapore's gorgeous beaches and tropical surroundings offer various possibilities for outdoor recreation and water sports. Swimsuits, board shorts, and cover-ups are ideal beachwear for going to the beach or partaking in recreational activities. Outside approved beach areas, modesty and respect must be maintained by avoiding revealing swimwear.

Tipping and Service Charges

Service Charges:
Many Singapore restaurants, hotels, and spas automatically add a service charge to the bill. This service charge, generally 10% to 15% of the total payment, is a tip for the employees. It is vital to underline that this pricing is not imposed but follows a well-known industry standard. As a result, tipping, in addition to the service charge, is uncommon.

Tipping in Restaurants and Cafes:
While it is not expected, leaving a tiny tip in restaurants and cafes is acceptable, especially if you enjoyed excellent

service and would like to express your gratitude. However, it is vital to realize that tipping is not a prevalent custom in Singapore, and most residents still need to leave extra gratuities. If you want to tip, a modest amount is sufficient, such as rounding up the total or leaving extra cash.

Hotel gratuities include the following:
It is frequent in hotels to come into instances when tipping is appropriate, mainly if you obtain specialized services or support from hotel staff. As a gesture of appreciation for their outstanding service, bellhops, housekeeping personnel, and concierge services may welcome a modest tip. While it is not obligatory, a simple payment of $1 to $5 is likely appropriate.

Tipping Tour Guides and Drivers:
Tipping tour guides is traditional as a token of appreciation for their knowledge and skill. Similarly, if you hire a private driver or use a ride-hailing service, rounding up the fare or giving a tiny tip is an excellent way to show your thanks.

Etiquette and Cultural Sensitivity:
While tipping is not customary in Singapore, expressing gratitude and appreciation for outstanding service is always appreciated. Instead of monetary gifts, a genuine grin, a verbal "thank you," or an excellent review may serve to show your appreciation. Knowing and obeying local tipping standards and laws displays cultural knowledge and improve the experience.

Local Laws and Regulations
Strict Drug Laws:
Singapore has a zero-tolerance attitude when it comes to illegal narcotics. Possession, trafficking, or use of drugs such as marijuana can result in severe punishments such as incarceration and, in extreme situations, the death penalty. It is crucial to maintain attention and avoid any interaction with illegal substances.

Cleanliness and Pollution Rules are Carefully Enforced: Singapore is well-known for its clean and well-maintained environment. Littering in public settings, including parks, streets, and public transportation, is unlawful. Offenders may face substantial fines as well as community service. It is best to help keep the city clean and dispose of trash in designated bins.

Strict Laws on Chewing Gum:
Chewing gum is not sold or imported in Singapore. Chewing therapeutic gum, such as dental or nicotine gum, is lawful but requires a prescription from a pharmacist. To prevent legal complications, it is necessary to take caution and avoid importing considerable volumes of gum into the nation.

Public Behavior and Etiquette:
Singapore regards public order and cooperation highly. Public nudity, graffiti, public drinking, and other disruptive behaviors are all strictly prohibited. It is crucial to grasp local standards and have appropriate general manners.

Strict Bans on Smoking:

In Singapore, smoking is entirely forbidden. Smoking is prohibited in most interior public locations, including restaurants, bars, shopping malls, and public transit. There are designated smoking sites, but it is crucial that you stay in them and do not smoke in non-smoking areas.

Respect for Cultural and Religious Sensitivities:
Singapore is a multi-cultural city-state with numerous religions and cultural customs. It is crucial to respect these sensitivities and stick to local standards when visiting religious sites, such as removing shoes before entering specific temples or mosques, dressing modestly, and refraining from disruptive behavior during religious activities or festivities.

Transportation Laws:
Singapore's transportation networks are carefully regulated. It is crucial to respect ticketing laws, avoid fare evasion, and give up seats to persons in need when utilizing public transit. Jaywalking is likewise unlawful; for their protection, pedestrians should use marked crossings and respect traffic signals.

Safety and Security

Stay Alert and Be Aware of Your Surroundings:
Maintaining situational awareness is crucial for safety in any situation. Look for potential hazards, especially in a crowded environment or near a tourist destination. Excessive use of technology, for example, should be avoided because it could make you a target for theft or other illegal activities. Trust your intuition and be on the watch for weird behavior or people.

Safeguard Your Property:
Although Singapore is mainly crime-free, it is always advisable to be careful. Passports, wallets, and mobile electronics should all be kept safe. In public, keep your bags in front of you, zippers closed, and facing your body. Avoid showing off enormous sums of money or wearing expensive objects that may attract unwanted attention.

Utilize Reliable Transportation:
Singapore has a modern, safe, and trustworthy public transit system. Always utilize licensed drivers while taking taxis or utilizing ride-hailing services. Check the driver's identification and that the vehicle always matches the criteria. Tell a trustworthy friend or family member about your travel.

Respect Local Laws and Customs:
For your protection, Singapore has strict driving laws that must be followed. Pedestrians must utilize marked crosswalks and heed traffic signals. Avoid jaywalking or crossing speeding autos when there are no pedestrian crossings. When riding or using personal mobility devices, stay on designated paths and always wear a helmet for protection.

Local customs and laws must be followed:
Singapore has strong laws and regulations in place that are severely enforced. To prevent legal complications, understand local customs and observe the rules. It includes: Not littering.

Smoking in Permitted Areas.
Adhering to chewing gum and drug regulations.

Stay Hydrated and Protect Yourself from the Sun:
In Singapore's hot and humid tropical climate, staying hydrated is crucial. Carry a water bottle with you throughout the day to keep hydrated. Wear sunscreen, a hat, and sunglasses to protect yourself from the sun. Seek shade during the warmest hours of the day to avoid heat exhaustion or sunburn.

Emergency Contacts and Assistance:
Learn Singapore's emergency phone numbers, such as 999 for police and 995 for ambulance services. Please notify the proper authorities or seek assistance from local businesses or neighbors if you require assistance.

CHAPTER THIRTEEN

Special Events and Festivals

Chinese New Year (CNY):

One of Singapore's most regularly observed holidays is the Chinese New Year commemorating the beginning of the lunar year. The city comes to life with sparkling decorations, lion and dragon dances, and bustling Chinatown streets. Families meet for extravagant feasts, trade crimson money gifts (ang baos), and revel in the joyous spirit. The Chingay Parade, which features spectacular floats, acrobatics, and cultural displays, adds to the festivities' magnificence.

Thaipusam:

Thaipusam is a fascinating Hindu holiday celebrated by Tamil to commemorate Lord Murugan, the deity of victory and battle. Pilgrims carry exquisite Kavadis (ornate metal constructs embellished with flowers and peacock feathers) and engage in religious activities like hooking and spearing their bodies. The procession from Sri Srinivasa Perumal Temple to Sri Thendayuthapani Temple is breathtaking, demonstrating the devotees' everlasting faith and fortitude.

Hari Raya Puasa:

Hari Raya Puasa, also known as Eid al-Fitr, marks the completion of Ramadan, the Islamic holy month of fasting. Malay people observe this occasion by worshiping, feasting, and visiting family and friends. The crowded bazaars selling Malay cuisine, clothes, and seasonal decorations bring Geylang Serai to life. The Ramadan

Light-Up adds to the festive ambiance by illuminating the streets with colorful lights and unique displays.

Deepavali:

Deepavali, also known as the Festival of Lights, is a well-known Hindu event that praises the triumph of virtue over evil and light over darkness. Little India has been transformed into a dazzling rainbow, complete with brilliant light shows, garlands, and gorgeous kolam (colorful rice flour motifs) covering the streets. Deepavali is a beautiful celebration with cultural performances, traditional attire and jewelry purchases, and excellent Indian cuisine.

Singapore Food Festival:

Singapore celebrates the annual Singapore Food Festival, a fascinating spectacle highlighting the city's many gastronomic delights as a nation with a rich culinary legacy. Food carts, pop-up restaurants, and celebrity chef collaborations merge great regional cuisines with imaginative inventions. The festival promotes Singapore's varied cuisines, from hawker areas to Michelin-starred restaurants, allowing food lovers to explore the city's culinary secrets.

Singapore Grand Prix:

The Formula 1 Singapore Grand Prix is an exciting race that provides high-speed racing to the city's heart. The Marina Bay Street track has been rebuilt into a magnificent promenade surrounded by noteworthy landmarks. Fans are drawn by the intense racing beneath the city's fantastic cityscape, star-studded performances, and world-class entertainment.

Singapore International Film Festival:
The Singapore Foreign Film Festival (SGIFF), a much-anticipated event that includes a broad range of local and foreign films, brings many filmgoers to Singapore. The festival highlights cinematic grandeur while fostering discourse and cultural interaction through screenings, seminars, and panel discussions. It helps the local film industry develop by creating a place for young filmmakers and talent.

Singapore Arts Festival:

The Singapore Arts Festival honors artistic expression and creativity by bringing together well-known local and international artists from various fields. The event comprises one-of-a-kind performances, exhibitions, and installations that challenge and stretch attendees' senses. The festival includes a diverse spectrum of intellectually fascinating cultural events, from theater and dance to visual arts and music.

CHAPTER FOURTEEN

Useful Phrases and Language Tips
Basic Phrases in Singaporean English

"Hello" and "Hi" are both appropriate greetings.
Thank you - "Thank you" or "Thanks."
"Ya" or "Yes" are both accurate.
"No" or "No lah" (a strong slang term)
Please - either "Please lah" or "Please."
Please excuse me - "Excuse me" or "Pardon me."
Sorry, both "sorry" and "sorry lah" are acceptable.
How are things going for you? - "How are you?" or "How are you doing?"
What is the address of...? "Where is...?"
Can you help me? "Can you help me?"
"I don't understand" and "I blur" are suitable expressions.
What is the cost? "How much does it cost?"
Delicious - "Delicious" or "Shiok" (overjoyed exclamation)
Please pass the bill to me. "Can I have the bill, please?" or "Can I have the check?"
Cheers! A typical Chinese toast is "Yam Seng!" or "Cheers!"
The phrase "Good morning" is used to greet someone.
Greetings - "Good afternoon."
Have a terrific day - "Have a nice day."

Singlish expressions

Lah is a word that can be used to emphasize or soften a statement. For example, "Don't be late, lah!"

Is it even possible? This phrase is used to ask if something is practical or practicable. "Can we meet at 6 p.m., or should we not?"

Alamak is a Turkish term that implies "surprise" or "dissatisfaction." "Alamak, I forgot to bring my umbrella!" for example.

Shiok: This word describes anything nice, tasty, or gratifying. For example, "The food at that hawker center is shook!"

Makan is Malay for "to eat" and is frequently used in Singlish. As in, "Let's go makan at the hawker center."

Blur-like sotong: This word conveys confusion or perplexity regarding something. "He's blurring like a sotong during the presentation."

To "chop" anything means to keep it for one's purpose. "For example," you might remark, "I'm going to chop this seat while you order the food."

Kiasu refers to the fear of missing out or being extremely competitive. "He's so kiasu," adds one, "always rushing to be the first in line."

Can-lah - A favorable reaction to a request or idea. "Can we go to the beach?" "Can-lah, let's do it!"

It's simply too pricey! - An exclamation expressing surprise or dismay over a high price. "Wow, the price of this handbag is exorbitant!"

Paiseh - is used to show grief or to apologize. "I sincerely apologize for being late, Paiseh."

Participate in a humorous or informal debate or share anecdotes that may or may not be entirely accurate. "He likes to talk cocky and make everyone laugh."

Catch no ball: This expression suggests being bewildered or unable to understand anything. "Sorry, I didn't catch the ball; please explain it again?"

Walao - is an exclamation of surprise, discontent, or annoyance. For example, "Walao, why is the train so crowded?"

Sabo - Sabo is a word that means to undermine or cause trouble for another person. "He sabo-ed me by giving me the wrong directions."

CONCLUSION

"Singapore Travel Guide 2023: A Comprehensive Guide to the City's Top Attractions" promises to be your go-to resource for viewing the richness of this expanding city-state. We have taken you on a fascinating journey throughout this tour, providing vital insights, insider suggestions, and extensive information about Singapore's must-see attractions.

We visited several locales that exemplify Singapore's distinctive blend of history and modernity, from the world-famous Marina Bay Sands to the scenic Gardens by the Bay, from the cultural enclaves of Chinatown and Little India to the historical landmarks of the Civic District.

Our detailed coverage of Singapore's major attractions has assisted you in designing a fantastic itinerary based on your tastes. Whether interested in history, gourmet cuisine, adventure, or culture, Singapore has something for you.

Walking through the streets of Singapore will wow you with its architectural marvels, enthrall you with its unique gastronomy scene, and enchant you with its rich cultural history. Singapore promises an immersive experience unlike any other, with everything from tasty local delicacies at hawker stalls to world-class museums and galleries highlighting the country's history and art.

Our travel guide also provides valuable information on transit, accommodation, gastronomy, and shopping to ensure your holiday runs well without hiccups. We've included practical recommendations to help you manage the city's efficient public transportation system, find the finest locations to stay based on your budget and interests, enjoy the city's excellent cuisine, and discover the vibrant retail areas that cater to every shopper's demands.

As you wave farewell to Singapore, we hope our travel guide has enriched your vacation and helped you make lasting memories in this magnificent city. Singapore never ceases to amaze. However, its major attractions are simply the tip of the iceberg.

Remember to immerse yourself in local culture, mingle with friendly locals, and take advantage of Singapore's unique experiences. Singapore will leave an unforgettable mark on your heart, whether a quiet stroll along the Marina Bay coastline, a culinary excursion through the hawker zones, or observing the stunning light shows and festivals.

Thank you for trusting "Singapore Travel Guide 2023" as your holiday companion. May your journey be filled with adventure, discovery, and the joy of seeing one of Asia's most beautiful sites. Have a safe flight and a happy stay in Singapore.